Whips of the West

An Illustrated History of American Whipmaking

THE BULLWHACKER OF THE PLAINS.

Bullwhacker of the Plains. This sketch of a bullwhacker is from *The Pacific Tourist,* edited by F. E.Shearer, published by J. R. Bowman, New York, 1882-83. The text indicated that the handle was no more than three feet in length, but the lash seldom less than twenty feet long. The lash tapered out from the butt for about six feet to a circumference of about ten inches, then tapered down to the point, where it finishes with a ribbon-shaped strand. The whips varied considerably depending upon the preferences of the user and what was available to him.

Whips of the West

An Illustrated History of American Whipmaking

David W. Morgan

Cornell Maritime Press
Centreville, Maryland 21617

Library of Congress Cataloging-in-Publication Data
Morgan, David W., 1925-
    Whips of the West : an illustrated history of American whipmak-
ing /
David W. Morgan.
        p. cm.
    Includes bibliographical references.
    ISBN 978-0-87033-589-1 (alk. paper)
                    1. Whips--West (U.S.) I. Title.
                        TS1040.M595 2007
                        685--dc22
                                        2006102661

Manufactured in the United States of America
First Edition; first printing, 2007

Table of Contents

Illustrations

Preface

This book is a history of the development of whips in the United States during the movement west into the plains, including the times generally known as the Old West. It is a compilation of the information I have acquired during forty years in whipmaking, and reflects a technical and analytical approach based on practical experience. I have not attempted a full academic survey of the literature and museum holdings, but have left this for someone else who may wish to build on the base I have laid. I hope this information also will be useful to museums in their understanding and presentation of their whip collections.

I have acknowledged those who contributed much in my earlier book *Whips and Whipmaking*, Second Edition. Here, I should like to mention those who have been particularly helpful in this study, E. Seyboldt, G. L. Soreghen, C. A. Cook, R. C. Nicoll, W. H. Scott, C. Shepperd, T. M. Kerr, and, specifically with reference to the buggy whips, Carol Marten and Robert Brown. My daughter Meredith read the manuscript and my son Will assisted with coordination and presentation. Many others have been generous in general or casual conversations with information and assistance through these many years, and I would like to thank them all.

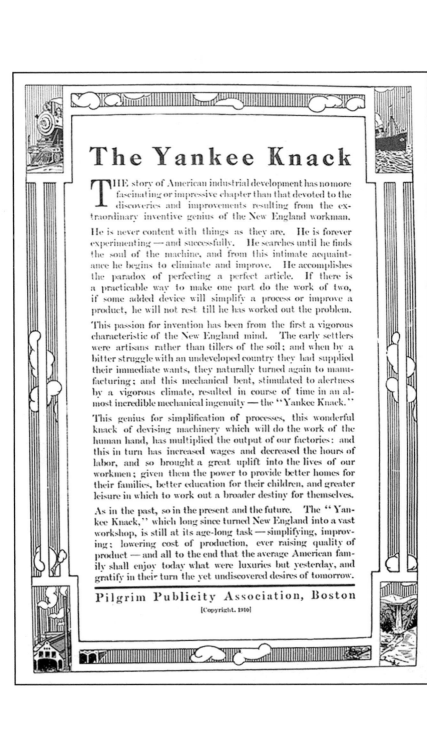

The Yankee Knack

THE story of American industrial development has no more fascinating or impressive chapter than that devoted to the discoveries and improvements resulting from the extraordinary inventive genius of the New England workman.

He is never content with things as they are. He is forever experimenting — and successfully. He searches until he finds the soul of the machine, and from this intimate acquaintance he begins to eliminate and improve. He accomplishes the paradox of perfecting a perfect article. If there is a practicable way to make one part do the work of two, if some added device will simplify a process or improve a product, he will not rest till he has worked out the problem.

This passion for invention has been from the first a vigorous characteristic of the New England mind. The early settlers were artisans rather than tillers of the soil; and when by a bitter struggle with an undeveloped country they had supplied their immediate wants, they naturally turned again to manufacturing; and this mechanical bent, stimulated to alertness by a vigorous climate, resulted in course of time in an almost incredible mechanical ingenuity — the "Yankee Knack."

This genius for simplification of processes, this wonderful knack of devising machinery which will do the work of the human hand, has multiplied the output of our factories; and this in turn has increased wages and decreased the hours of labor, and so brought a great uplift into the lives of our workmen; given them the power to provide better homes for their families, better education for their children, and greater leisure in which to work out a broader destiny for themselves.

As in the past, so in the present and the future. The "Yankee Knack," which long since turned New England into a vast workshop, is still at its age-long task — simplifying, improving; lowering cost of production, ever raising quality of product — and all to the end that the average American family shall enjoy today what were luxuries but yesterday, and gratify in their turn the yet undiscovered desires of tomorrow.

Pilgrim Publicity Association, Boston

Introduction

This is the story of opening up the West from a different viewpoint—that of the whips that urged on the horses and oxen, controlled cattle on the open range, and kept them moving through the stockyards. These whips are American whips, derived from the whips of Mongolia or Europe, used side by side with whips from Australia and England, but uniquely American, showing the innovative improvement in production and the strong individualistic spirit of the 1800s that originated in New England and is still alive in the West.

To understand these whips, it is necessary to look back at the history of settlement, to the beginnings of the western movement in the early 1800s and before. The population was expanding at a rate of more than 30 percent per year throughout the first half of the century, with cities such as New York, Boston, and Philadelphia growing quickly and establishing industries. The need for foodstuffs increased, both for domestic consumption and export, giving incentive for development of the fertile and productive lands beyond the Allegheny Mountains. The industrial revolution in England brought with it new possibilities for industry and changing outlooks. Education, particularly in New England, was becoming universal, allowing more people to take advantage of new opportunities in industry, agriculture, and trade.

In colonial times, horsewhips usually consisted of a hickory stick with a single strand of leather or a braided thong of leather attached, often made by the user. Carriage whips and the shorter chaise whips had a holly stick, and were imported from England or made by immigrant English whipmakers. The rapid increase in population in the 1800s, and the improvement in transportation with turnpikes, macadamized roads, canals, and railroads, created a demand for buggy whips and horse whips.

Production of buggy whips developed in Westfield, Massachusetts to the extent that they could call themselves the "whip city of the world." It is a good example of how the industrial revolution grew in America. In the industrial revolution production of goods moved from small shops of skilled craftsmen or home production, to large industrial operations using machinery and power assistance and less skilled workers.

The industrial revolution started in England in the last half of the eighteenth century, but had little effect in the United States at the time, because the American Revolution and the French-English wars inhibited communication with England. The fruits of the industrial revolution in England became more available in America after the French-English wars ended with the Battle of Waterloo in 1815, and Americans could more readily travel to England. The English government tried to restrict export of technology, but was not entirely successful, and could not restrict knowledge of the basic concepts.

The movement from craft work to factory production in the United States took place mainly in New England. Two factors were behind this, education and a labor force of wage workers. Education for all was established in New England long before it occurred in the Mid-Atlantic or southern states. The work force in New England consisted largely of wage workers, rather than the slaves and indentured servants of the southern and Mid-Atlantic states. Labor was also in short supply, and as a consequence wages were high and workers could move readily between jobs or different trades, gaining wider experience. Industry became much more open, and this environment of educated workers created a "can-do" attitude of enterprise that came to be known as the "Yankee Knack" or "Yankee Enterprise." The key factors in the Yankee Knack were organization of factory production of large quantities of similar items, and the use of specialized machinery. With good organization and a clearly defined process, the advantages of specialized machines became clear and the cost of development could be justified. The quality and finish of the best craftwork was not always attained, but a reliable quality could be mass produced.

The Yankee Knack did not stop in New England, but continued with the western movement. The Diamond Whip Company of Chicago braided bull whips and lashes on machines, and, more recently, in 1960, Eugene O'Neill set up the Wonder Whip Company in Fostoria, Iowa, making straight-out whips with a fiberglass core. In the West, Main & Winchester of San Francisco maintained a strong regional operation in hand-braided whips, not fully mechanized, but highly organized in production and sales. Craft work continued in the West with individual whipmakers and saddlers, who made regional patterns or general patterns that competed with the Main & Winchester and Diamond Whip Company whips.

Chapter 1

Population and the Movement West

The population of the United States grew very rapidly in the first half of the nineteenth century. The population was 5,308,483 in 1800 and 23,191,876 in 1850. Before 1750, the population had been located largely on the eastern seaboard, adjacent to water, either rivers or estuaries, wherever a safe harbor was possible. Transportation had been largely by water. Overland transportation had been effectively limited to individuals using horses or walking. Overland freight had been moved by packhorses or farm wagons using slow, heavy horses. This pattern only changed after 1800, when better roads and later canals and railroads were developed.

Patterns of immigration and settlement differed in the different regions of the country. The South, with a plantation economy, was split between rich slave-owning plantation owners and poor white immigrants who were largely Scots-Irish of Northern Ireland or from northern England. The plantation owners, who controlled the government, did not support education for either slaves or the poor whites (Sowell 2005). The Mid-Atlantic region had been settled by English from the south of England, but the working population was largely made up of slaves and indentured servants. New England was settled by the Pilgrims, Quakers, and Unitarians, all of whom were educated and in favor of education for all. Massachusetts, and New England in general, were more egalitarian than were the Mid-Atlantic or southern states. The working population in New England was made up primarily of wage workers, with few slaves and indentured servants. The workers were in short supply, could change jobs readily, and could return to farming if they wished. After the wars in Europe were settled, German immigrants came to New England, often passing through on their way to the West. They too were usually educated.

Early migration west to the plains was largely from the South, through Kentucky and Tennessee to Indiana and southern Illinois. After the Erie Canal, which connected the Hudson River to the Great Lakes, was opened in 1825, New England and the northeast region became the main source for migrants to the West, and the Erie Canal became central to transport of the products of the plains.

America at this time had an open agricultural frontier. Food for the increasing population on the eastern seaboard was produced on newly developed farmland further west. The northeast developed as the main commercial region, with a strong base in shipbuilding and trade with Europe, and secondary support businesses such as financing and insurance. As the northeast became urbanized and industrialized, the movement west for farmland grew, and the need for better transportation became imperative. Without reliable transportation, grain could not be readily brought to market. Grain could be fed to pigs that could be driven to market or converted to whisky, a high-value item that could be shipped. The amount of grain that could be produced as people moved west far exceeded the shipping capacity to take the grain to the East Coast population centers.

Land transportation had remained the main bottleneck to expansion throughout the country (Dunbar 1937). Tracks using packhorses were widened to allow wheeled vehicles around 1750, and the Conestoga wagon developed as the prime freight vehicle. Pennsylvania did not have the natural waterways found in other states, and was at the forefront of developing roads. The early roads were passable during dry weather but became mudholes during wet weather. They were somewhat improved by putting small logs side by side across them, forming corduroy roads. During winter in the colder areas, sleds became the common and most practical mode of overland travel. Turnpikes, roads on which charges were made for passage, were built in increasing numbers, but little improvement in the roads took place until the introduction of macadamized roads around 1830. These roads, developed by a Scottish engineer John L. McAdam, were constructed on a base of stones with smaller stones and gravel on top, cambered to let water run off. This construction was a major improvement and permitted easy movement of wheeled vehicles during all weather. Eventually, tar was applied to seal the surface, which further improved the surface and durability of the road and reduced dust in dry weather. The construction then became known as "tarmac."

The establishment of good roads and turnpikes gave rise to a rapid increase in the number of wheeled vehicles, both for freight and people. Roads were extended inside the towns and cities, increasing the number of carriages and chaises.

Canals were also built in this period. They were a major improvement for shipping freight, but did not reduce the use of wagons and carts, since the latter were needed at any terminus to carry the goods to or from the canal boats. A surge in building and improving waterways and building new canals occurred between 1820 and 1830. Of particular importance was the Erie Canal, which linked the eastern seaboard to Lake Erie. The population of New York doubled following the opening of the Erie Canal, showing the effect of increased trade.

The canals were both extended and supplanted by the construction of the railways, which began in the 1830s. While railway construction was developed earlier in Britain, development of steam power and railroads had been progressing along similar lines in the United States, and once development started the railroads

BEFORE THE RAILROAD. SIX HORSE FREIGHT TEAM, CASTA. ALTA.

Figure 1.1. Six-horse freight team. The horse teams that hauled freight before the railroad continued after the railroad was built, when they turned to taking freight to and from the railroad depots.

Whips of the West

expanded quickly. State and city governments encouraged railroads with exclusive rights and direct financing, and capital from England helped fuel a dramatic boom in railroad building. When canal and rail transport reached Chicago and the Mississippi River, trade through the Northeast increased because goods that previously had been shipped down the Mississippi for export to Europe could be shipped by rail and canal to the eastern seaboard. Migration through New York and New England to the fertile fields of Illinois and the west also increased accordingly. The McCormick reaper, developed in 1831, greatly reduced the labor requirements of the grain farms and permitted rapid expansion of the grain supply. In 1847 McCormick moved his production facility from Virginia to Chicago, where he could increase production. The Midwest region, and Chicago in particular, expanded greatly as railroads extended to the plains to handle the grain trade. Railroads soon fanned out west from Chicago, bringing not only grain to the rail terminals, but cattle and pigs to a growing number of slaughterhouses. Shipment of grain and flour grew rapidly both for domestic use in the East Coast population centers and for export to Britain and Europe (Licht 1995). The pattern of transportation had been established for continuing movement west into the short-grass prairie and beyond.

Chapter 2

The Industrial Revolution in America

The industrial revolution started in England about the middle of the eighteenth century, but did not affect America significantly until much later. The American Revolution and the French-English wars restricted communication and transfer of technology until the wars were settled at Waterloo in 1815. The English, hoping to maintain their export trade, attempted to prevent export of either machines or other technology, but were generally unsuccessful because of personal connections between Americans and the English and emigration of knowledgeable English workers. Early development of industry in America took place largely in New England, rather than the Mid-Atlantic or southern states. This was determined by the character and culture of the population. Three factors stand out in this, education, the preponderance of wage workers, and an egalitarian attitude.

Education in New England was better than the other regions both in terms of quality and the proportion of the population served, and the working classes had a sound practical education. Education not only gave workers a better appreciation of the crafts in which they might engage, but also gave them more confidence in improving the operation. Employing wage workers rather than the slaves or indentured servants, coupled with a general shortage of workers, allowed workers to change jobs readily and to move between industries or trades. The workers also often came from a farm background, and since land was cheap they could return or go to farming if they desired, which gave them the confidence to change jobs. The net effect was that the workers were widely knowledgeable within their trade, although possibly less skilled at any specific operation, confident of their abilities, and accepting of machines that could reduce their labor. An egalitarian attitude in New England allowed a productive transfer of the experience of the workforce to management, unhampered by tradition or craft restrictions, which allowed workers to set up independently to develop production. Significant numbers of women were employed in factories or as home workers for the factories. Labor was short, and women from the small family farms were keen to work for wages, though they were paid less than men. The small farms required heavy labor for the most part, and women were often under-employed. Development of purpose-built machines for the factory or home use gave new opportunities for employing women.

Low food costs and higher disposable income among the rural middle class, who could now be reached by improved transportation, contributed to the rapid expansion of the American consumer market. Additional factors in promoting the industrial revolution in New England were the availability of streams suitable for producing power for factories, and a ready availability of capital, both on a small scale from the workers who were relatively well paid, and on a larger scale from the merchant class and the shipping industry.

The key to the development of industry in New England became known as the Yankee Knack, so clearly was this development seen as beyond that of other regions. Two factors were central, organizing a process for quantity production of an item or class of item, and use of specialized machinery. By organizing a process into clearly defined steps, the advantage of specialized machinery became clear and the cost of development could be justified. The openness of industry aided the development of secondary industry designing and manufacturing specialized machinery, which in turn assisted other developing industries. The growth of the buggy whip industry in Westfield, Massachusetts is a good example of this aspect of the industrial revolution in America.

Chapter 3
The Buggy Whip Industry

Buggy whips include both the simple straight-out whip with a cracker or popper on the end, and also the drop-top whips with a thong on the end made either as an extension of the braided cover of the whip or as a separate thong. All were made in immense variety.

Production of buggy whips developed in Westfield, Massachusetts, and is a good example of the development of industry from a craft to factory production as part of the industrial revolution in New England. A detailed survey of the industry in Westfield was published in 1891 (Appendix A), and a later history in 1910 (Appendix B). The whip industry in Westfield started in 1808 with a Joseph Jokes. He had hickory on his property with which he made whip stocks, and attached a simple leather lash. The thongs were braided from strips of leather. Initially the strips were cut with the leather lying on a table, a common and continuing American practice for heavy hides. Later, the strands were cut by drawing the leather through a set of knives, a method attributed to the Shakers of Lebanon, New Hampshire. Morell Baker Jr., who distributed seeds, and included whips among the items he carried, established a better way of making whips in the early 1800s (Sommer 1972). This method was faster and cheaper than cutting individual strands, although it did not lend itself well to producing a tapered thong for whips.

In Australia, two sets of knives set at different separations were used to give the strands a rough taper. The thongs were finished by rolling with white soap. By 1820 others, presumably immigrant English whipmakers, were making stocks of rattan cane and whalebone in Westfield, which were covered with braided cotton thread. The first efforts in braiding covers were by hand, with bobbins sus-

Fig. 3.1. Fringe Cutter. This machine cut fringed leathers for bats.

pended around a barrel, as had been done earlier in England. Later, Hiram Hull saw a machine plaiting shoelaces in Providence and, recognizing the potential value to the whip industry, bought the patent rights. He then developed a braiding machine to braid the covers on the whips.

The development of braiding machines, although unknown in Westfield in the early years, was well advanced in England and Germany, and braiding machines were imported and adapted to use in Westfield. Recognizing the value of an invention abroad and adapting or improving it to suit an American operation was more typical of the Yankee Knack than inventing a new process. With the newly adapted braiding machines, the buggy whip industry changed from a craft industry to a factory industry.

The industry in Westfield was competitive and well organized. Those in the industry were capable of recognizing useful techniques and developing specialized machines. The industry grew, (making about three million whips per year at its peak), and was large enough to spawn secondary support industries. Westfield became a center of industry, continually improving design and process.

The early composite whip stocks were made using whalebone (Ashford 2004). Whalebone, or baleen, the flexible horn-like mate-

Fig. 3.2. Flat-bed braiding machine. Thread covers are put on the buggy whips with this flat-bed braiding machine. The core is put down through the floor, and is drawn back up as the cover is braided into place.

rial that makes up the filtration system for some whales, was the common spring material before spring steel and resilient plastics were developed. Strips of whalebone were soaked in a brook for four or five weeks to soften. They were then steamed to soften them further and rived into separate strips. The strips were shaped by hand using a hand plane and formed into a tapered assembly that was stuck together with pitch. A braided cover of gut, thread, or leather was put over this assembly.

Full whalebone stocks, formed from a number of tapered strips of whalebone, required skillful shaping of the whalebone by experienced craftsmen, and were expensive in terms of both labor and material. Whalebone became more expensive as excessive hunting reduced the whale population, and stocks with a single piece of whalebone surrounded by cane became standard. Cane strips were cut to fit around the whalebone (and later rawhide) and tied in place with string. This core was dipped in tar (and later glue) and

Fig. 3.3. English hunt thong foundation. This is a whalebone center foundation for an English hunt thong. It has a paper cover to smooth the surface and provide a foundation for the braided cover.

Fig. 3.4. Whalebone center crop. The whalebone in this English hunt crop has three pieces to get the required stiffness. The whalebone is stocked with cane and then wrapped with paper.

Fig. 3.5. String source for cane-stocked cores. The rotating cane stocked core assembly was run through this machine for its string binding.

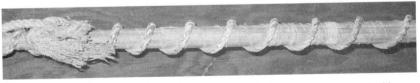

Fig. 3.6. Roped cane-stocked core. The cane-stocked cores are wrapped with string when they are assembled, then roped tightly with a small diameter rope before being dipped in tar or glue. The tight roping is necessary to bind the cane and whalebone or rawhide, whichever is used, to form a densely compact whole.

The Buggy Whip Industry

tied tightly with rope to compress it and make it solid. With further increases in the price of whalebone, spring steel rods were used in place of the whalebone. Steel made a durable center with the requisite elasticity, but could not be tapered, so the even bend required for the whip had to be determined by the cane around the steel center. The even bend could not always be obtained this way. An alternative center made of twisted rawhide was developed in Westfield. This proved most successful, and was a significant factor in putting the manufacture of whips on a firm factory basis. Strips of tapered rawhide were twisted to form a rough tapered round shape. This was then made smooth, at first by hand, and later by a special machine with two opposing grindstones set to work with an adjustable cam. This machine could make a very accurately tapered round, with good elastic and bending characteristics and desirable weight and balance. The rawhide was encased in cane, and the cane tapered accurately with a similar machine using disks with cutting knives. Such a well-made core reduced the need for later adjustment. The grindings from the rawhide were made into glue to hold the core together, replacing the pitch used earlier with whalebone centers. Before twisting, the rawhide strips were given shallow slits on one side to help them lay flatter when twisted and dried. The rawhide might be twisted around a piece of cane, but the core could be given more resilience and weight by twisting the rawhide around a steel center. For riding crops the rawhide was usually twisted around a small diameter length of cane that kept the crops from taking a permanent set if left leaning against a wall or otherwise distorted. The rawhide needed protection from moisture, which would soften it. The thread cover on the whip offered some protection, as did a braided eelskin or other cover, but a better seal from moisture was developed, using a coating of vulcanized rubber.

Rawhide centers were made in the whipmaking factories, but in 1888 a separate factory was set up by Turner and Cook in Southfield, Massachusetts, to make whip centers and rawhide belt pins for machinery belting. This factory made centers for the whip manufacturers, including some in England, and operated until 1977. The preferred rawhide for the whip cores was water buffalo. The tapered pieces for the cores were cut by hand, and put on a rack of thirty-six for twisting and drying. They were twisted around

Fig. 3.7. Machine for putting a partial slit in the rawhide to be twisted. The tapered rawhide to be twisted is given shallow slits on one side so that it will lay flatter when it is twisted and dried.

Fig. 3.8. Frame for twisting rawhide. The tapered rawhide strips are mounted on frames with a hook connection that can be twisted as the rawhide dries.

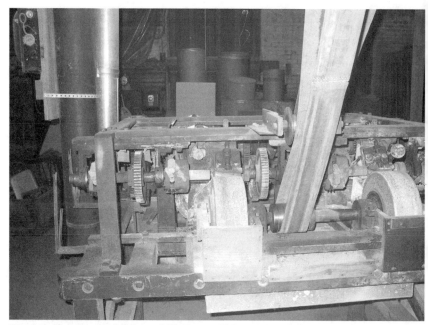

Fig. 3.9. Machine to finish rawhide cores. This machine takes the twisted rawhide core on a cam arrangement past two grindstones that finish the core on a taper. The finish is accurately done, well enough that crops were made with bare rawhide cores coated with a clear finish.

Fig. 3.10. Knives to finish cane-stocked cores. Cane-stocked cores were finished on a machine similar to that used for finishing the rawhide cores, but with the grindstones replaced with sets of knife blades mounted on rotating discs.

Fig. 3-11. Steel-center rawhide core. This steel center twisted rawhide core was made by Tom Hill in Australia for riding crops. It was durable and provided good flex and weight. It was hand finished, and lacked the fine surface finish of the American cores finished by machine. It was covered in paper before a braided kangaroo skin overlay was put on.

Fig. 3.12. Cutting rawhide for centers. The tapered strips of rawhide for the twisted centers were cut on a table with a straight knife, tapered by eye. Courtesy W. Scott.

a piece of rattan about two-thirds the length of the rawhide. The drying cores were again twisted during drying to keep them tightly twisted. The grinding machine to finish the twisted rawhide was developed in the early 1900s. This machine gave the cores an accurate taper and a fine finish. The cores were used in buggy whips and riding crops. The finish was sufficiently fine that the cores were sometimes used in crops without a cover.

Fig. 3.13. Mounting rawhide strips. The tapered rawhide strips were stretched onto the frames. Courtesy W. Scott.

Fig. 3.14. Tightening rawhide twist. The drill for twisting the rawhide was on the end of a rod connected to a drive belt. Courtesy W. Scott.

The transition of whip manufacture from craft to factory production accompained the rapid expansion of the market as population and roads expanded. The market was extremely competitive. A long stick or a rough thong on a hickory stick would urge on a horse as well as a whip made by a craftsman or in a factory, but these were not compatible with a good turn-out of matched horses and an expensive carriage. Buggy whips became a fashion item. The English had long developed high-quality whips as a status item in driving carriages and American producers were quick to follow their lead. The factories were capable of expanding production to a degree that the craft shops were not, making a variety of styles in a wide range of prices, and encouraging customers to consider the whip as a significant item in their equipage. While it might seem counterproductive to produce a range of styles in a factory built on the premise of cost savings in mass producing a single item, the styles could still take advantage of the specialized machines. The added requirement was organization, at which the American factories excelled. The buggy whip factories also produced a variety of braided leather items, and braided leather covers for crops and whip handles. Bullwhips, team whips, dog whips, and horse gear were manufactured.

Whips of the West

Fig. 3.15. Drive for tightening rawhide twist. The factory was run on belts and pulleys, including the drill for twisting the rawhide. Turner and Cook also made pins for joining the leather belts used in factories. Courtesy W. Scott.

The Buggy Whip Industry

Fig. 3.16. Marble slab roller for leather braids. This rolling setup was used to roll braided leather items.

Hickory whip stocks for horse whips generally remained a craft item. The better quality were shaved, but cheaper stocks were turned. Shaved stocks followed the grain better than did turned stocks, and were stronger and more reliable. A center for this trade was among the German community in Milford Township, Bucks County, Pennsylvania (*The Carriage Journal* 1973).

The availability of inexpensive factory-made whips did not eliminate horse whips or thongs made by the user, nor using a length of twig or sapling cut from the brush as a straight-out whip. When farmers in Canada moved further west to a new farm, they would take shoots of red willow with them to plant at the new farm for a supply of buggy whips.

Unlike their American counterparts, the English whipmakers did not have a fast-growing domestic market. They had an established export market in America, and produced a wide range of buggy whips, but did not expand to take full advantage of the American market. Although they used braiding machines, they did not develop the specialized machinery for tapering cores or rawhide centers, which eventually they imported from America. They continued basically as craft shops, following traditional ways. The workers were poorly paid and had little prospect of moving to a new or better job. The owners were generally separated from the workers by distinctions of money and class, and competitive entry into the trade was not encouraged. Poor communication between workers and owners hindered improvement. In the United States, the movement from craft to factory accompanied employment of women operating purpose-built machines, either in factories or at home as outworkers on piecework. Insignificant numbers of women were employed in the industry in England, where whip-making remained a craft operation.

Holly whips and finely finished whips continued to be imported from England, as the American whips lacked the extreme quality of the best craft whips, settling short of this for reliability. Although holly whips were made in America by immigrant craftsmen, the quality of English grown holly was superior, possibly enhanced by the long experience of the English whipmakers in selecting the best holly from the best environment and regions. Holly whips were made also in American factories with sticks imported from England. The holly was worked on a lathe with a shaped cutter, rather than with rasps and files as in England. Sanding was done on a lathe, with a final hand rubbing.

The wide range of whips made is illustrated in the catalog of the Cargill, Cleveland and Company, reproduced in Appendix C. They were one of the large whip producers and offered a full range of whips, including team whips, drover whips, quirts and dog whips, buggy whips, and carriage whips. Buggy whips could be all cane or with different cores and centers of whalebone, steel, or rawhide. The rawhide used could be of different origins to give different properties or, possibly of more importance, better advertising opportunities. Rawhide whips could be protected from moisture with a rubber cover. Additional undercovers could be made of spring steel wire to enhance both resilience and weight. Ornamentation was important to all the whips, including the lower-priced models. A stream of new models was necessary to keep each producer competitive, and whips came to be sold to suit regional preferences or groups.

The buggy whip industry decreased rapidly with the development of automobiles, although 1910, eight years after the Duryea brothers introduced the first single cylinder horseless carriage in Springfield, Massachusetts, was the year of maximum sales for the industry.

Westfield, Massachusetts was the center of the whipmaking industry, and at its peak was home to more than forty companies making whips or parts for whips. The largest of these, the U.S. Whip Company, employed more than 300 workers and shipped more than 100,000 finished whips per week. U.S. Whip had a second factory in Ohio and sales offices throughout the United States and Europe.

The only whip company still surviving is the Westfield Whip Manufacturing Company, started by Harold Martin in 1946. Harold Martin was able to build his new venture, even as others were closing, by capitalizing on the large quantity of backorders that had accumulated during the Second World War. By 1948 Westfield Whip Manufacturing Company had acquired most of the whip companies that had remained in business after the war, and in 1951 they completed the process by buying the one remaining competitor, Cargill, Cleveland & Company. Martin moved his operation into the Cargill, Cleveland & Company building, built in the 1880s, where his company still operates today.

In 1960, Eugene O'Neill set up the Wonder Whip Company in Fostoria, Iowa. His background was in retailing horse equipment and Western wear, with no experience in whipmaking. He started by pushing fiberglass rods through a braided synthetic rope, and patented a method of attaching the snap or popper to the end. In the 1980s he upgraded his production by braiding the whip cover onto the fiberglass core. These whips found a ready market in harness racing. O'Neill was very aggressive in marketing and the company grew very quickly. He obstructed competition by buying all the braiding machines he could find on the market. Any he could not use he destroyed and personally took to the dump. He retired in the 1990s, sold his company, and moved to Australia.

Under Harold Martin, Westfield Whip Manufacturing Company continued to manufacture a full range of whips using rawhide and rattan, and later synthetic cores. The technology had evolved since the early days, and some of the changes are documented in the pamphlet by Harold Martin, reproduced in Appendix D. At the

Fig. 3.17. Westfield Whip Mfg. Co. Ltd. building. The Westfield Whip building is listed with the Department of the Interior National Park Service on the National Register of Historic Places. It was built ca. 1887 by A. G. Barnes Whip Company, which became the Massasoit Whip Company. It was purchased in 1893 by the U.S. Whip Company, which added several single-story additions. It was purchased in 1910 by Rogers Silver Co., which rented space to several small whip companies. From 1923 to 1928 it was owned by Barry Whip Co., Cargill, Cleveland & Co., Swiss American Watch Co., and Henry J. Miller Co. About 1928 Cargill, Cleveland became sole owner, and sold it in 1951 to H. J. Martin at the Westfield Whip Company.

time the pamphlet was written, Turner and Cook in Southfield, Massachusetts was still producing most of the rawhide cores used by Westfield Whip, sized to their specifications. Turner and Cook ceased operations in 1977, and while Westfield Whip still produces whips with rawhide cores, in the late 1970s the company began to manufacture more whips using man-made materials for cores than rawhide. Their experience with the older rawhide cores has proven invaluable in allowing Westfield Whip to design cores in man-made materials to give the needed properties for each whip they make.

Westfield Whip is now run by Harold Martin's daughter, Carol, and her business partner Dan Seals. They still use the historic equipment and specialized machines designed for whipmaking in Westfield more than a century ago, but while they still can produce rawhide whips, the cost is prohibitive. Suitable rawhide is difficult to obtain. Water buffalo hide is not readily available and rawhide from cows generally comes from feedlots where growth stimulants result in hides of inferior quality.

Westfield Whip Manufacturing Company is an unusual link with the industrial history of New England not only because they are the only survivor of the once-flourishing buggy whip industry, but because they have retained so much of the older equipment and the knowledge of how it was used. They also have an archive of records from their predecessor, the Cargill Cleveland & Company dating in the 1880s. The building itself is listed on the National Register of Historic Places. Harold Martin had bought older type machinery from other whipmaking companies throughout the East Coast and Canada in hopes of developing a working museum to memorialize the whipmaking industry of Westfield. He amassed a collection of equipment from the early days of whipmaking unusual in degree, diversity, and scale for any industrial operation. Carol Martin is now inventorying this collection and the archive of records as a start toward establishing a working museum that would retain this unique link and make it available to the public.

Chapter 4
Wagon Whips and Oxen Whips

A variety of whips have been used with cattle, horses, and mules. These were usually heavier than buggy whips: muleskinners' whips, stock whips, wagon whips, or oxen (bullock) whips. In the early days these whips were made largely by users, small craft shops, or saddlers. Bark whips were made by users on farms, primarily for moving milk cows or for use with horses. Their overriding advantage was that they were cheap. John Quincy Wolf in the Department of English at Southwestern University in Memphis inquired in the Ozarks, Missouri, and Tennessee about bark whips and obtained samples, as well as recollections from the early 1900s. The whips were made in the spring, when the sap was rising, as the bark peeled more readily then. Paw paw was often preferred where available, otherwise hickory. Mulberry root was said to be used as well.

Fig. 4.1. Bark Whip with integral handle. The thong on this whip is made with bark stripped back to a short section of a secondary branch. The whip is thrown with the secondary branch trailing, so that the bark is not torn from the branch. The end of the secondary branch is wrapped with bark to help avoid the bark stripping back further. Courtesy Jon Quincy Wolf.

Fig. 4.2. Bark whip with separate handle. Bark whips were not uncommon on farms where cash was short and a better whip was not essential. This whip has a bark thong attached to a handle by a sling string. Bark whips could be kept in a water trough to keep them supple or they could be soaked in castor oil. Castor oil was used in doctoring cows (and people), and was a staple on farms. Courtesy John Quincy Wolf.

Whips were developed to meet regional or local needs and preferences. The wagoners in the early 1800s used a five-foot whip, thick at the butt, and tapering rapidly to a cracker at the end. T.B. Searight's *The Old Pike*, refers to Battley White of Centerville, Pennsylvania as having made more of these whips than any man on the road (Searight 1844). The center of his whip was rawhide. Searight also records John Morrow of Petersburg, Pennsylvania as making this type of whip.

A different style of wagon whip was the Loudon whip, made in Loudon, Pennsylvania. The butt section of this whip had a flexible wood center. Wagon whips could have a core of rawhide or solid leather, with a solid leather cover on the stock end, with a twisted or braided buck point, or with a braided cover or leather or rawhide, usually again with a buckskin point. The handle might be wire wrapped. Express whips were similar, but were longer, about seven to eight feet, including the 4½ feet stiffened butt section.

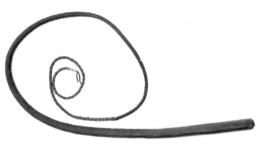

Fig. 4.3. Wagon whip. This whip has a sewn cover over a core of leather strips. The point is braided buckskin. The hand part is stiffened and weighted by an iron or steel insert, shown in Fig. 4.6. The strips in the core and the iron insert are shown in place at the butt of the whip in Fig. 4.5.

Fig. 4.4. Frayed end of wagon whip. The frayed end of this wagon whip shows the strands of leather used as a core.

Fig. 4.5. Butt end of wagon whip. The end of this wagon whip shows the leather strands making up the core and the iron piece used to stiffen and weight the hand part. A nail used to hold the end knot can be seen.

Fig. 4.6. Wagon whip showing end insert. An eight-inch length of iron, rectangular in cross section is inserted in the end of this wagon whip to stiffen the hand grip and weight the end. There had been knots at the end and six inches from the end defining the grip.

Elmer Seybold was a whipmaker who made whips for the oil fields. He was the only professional whipmaker in the early days of the Smackover, Arizona; Seminole, Oklahoma; Wink, Texas; and Kilgore, Texas oilfields. He had started making whips when he was nine years old, and was making a living with whips when he was twelve. He was very helpful in providing details and samples of the whips of that time (1920s). Since he followed traditional local usage, his work is indicative of earlier work in the East. The whips used were mainly muleskinners' and bullwhackers' (ox drivers') whips. The muleskinners, working from the box, used a whip with a thong about thirteen to fourteen feet long, and a handle 3½ to 4 feet long. On large teams a second muleskinner would work the boiler string, the six mules nearest the wagon, riding a mule next to the wagon and using a whip with a heavier, thirteen to fourteen feet thong and a shorter handle twelve to sixteen inches long. This whip was similar to the Florida Cow whip. The handles were hickory, shaved down to size. The longer handles were shaved down to where they flexed well and sometimes soaked in oil or buried in

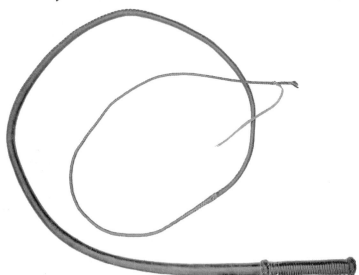

Fig. 4-7. Loudon wagon whip. The Loudon wagon whip was stiffened with a hickory insert under the first section of the sewn cover. The stiffening ran about three feet, followed by about three feet of leather core, and finally about three feet of braided buck point. The hand part was wrapped with copper wire in separated coils to improve the grip.

Whips of the West

Fig. 4.8. Loudon whip hand part. Copper wire was wound around the hand part of the Loudon whip to improve the grip. The wire would be wound tightly when the leather was wet in order to make a deep depression. This technique was used occasionally on other whips.

horse manure to make them more limber. The short-handles were fairly stiff. The same short handled whip was used by outriders assisting very large teams.

Muleskinners who worked only two mules were looked down upon by the others, and often made their whips out of trace leather, as a solid leather thong, seven to eight feet long. Many of these individuals were not full time muleskinners, but worked in the oilfields as "tie hackers," cutting railroad ties in the winter when there was nothing else to do.

Elmer Seybold made his whips of Indian-tan lace leather, four strands, with a buckskin or kangaroo point and a seagrass popper. The strands were cut straight the full length of the side, requiring that he splice strands to get the full length of the whip. The cowhide strands were cut without a taper. To taper them, one end was held in a vice and the strand tapered by running the strand through the hand with a knife to cut the strand. The pieces cut off in tapering the strand were used to form the core of the thong. He did not bevel the strands. The point of the whip was made in buckskin, or kangaroo when he could get it. The point was finished with a seagrass popper, usually twisted from two strands, but sometimes braided in four strands, which commanded a higher price.

The thong was attached to the handle by a sling string. This was done with a notch on the end of the handle for most whips, or a hole in the end of the handle coming out at the side, as in some Florida Cow whips. The notch was easier to make. The hole in the end was more commonly used in earlier times.

Bullock thongs were much heavier, and attached to a handle 5 to 5½ feet long. The teams were usually three yoke of oxen (six oxen), but sometimes as many as thirty oxen might be yoked together. The bullwhacker walked by the side of his wheelers (the rear yoke),

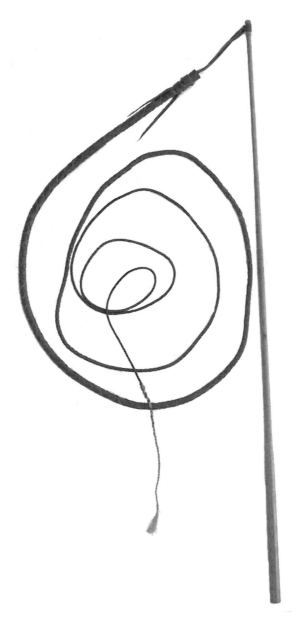

Fig. 4.9. Muleskinner's whip. This muleskinner's whip was made by Elmer
Seybold. The thong is cowhide, with a kangaroo hide point and a twisted sea
grass cracker. The handle is four feet long. Some muleskinners liked very heavy
whips. Mr. Seybold recalled making a thong with six fishing sinkers in the belly, an
extremely heavy whip but apparently to the liking of the owner.

Whips of the West

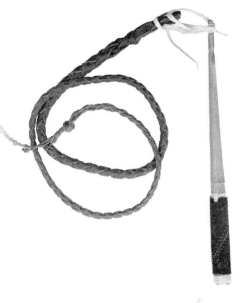

Fig. 4.10. Old muleskinner's whip. This is an old muleskinner's whip of the type used by farmers working one or two mules. The sling string is a replacement. The handle is sixteen inches long. These whips were often made by the users, and might be fairly crude.

Fig. 4.11. Whip for twelve-horse hitch. This is a reproduction made by Elmer Seybold of a whip he had made in 1926 for Dirty Vic Dunlap, who drove a 12-horse hitch for Ringling Brothers Circus. Dunlap used the original on a 4-foot whalebone stock. The thong is braided over a 13-foot length of 3/16th-inch vinyl covered cable. It starts out in a 6-plait cowhide, and finishes in kangaroo with a twisted sea grass cracker. Dunlap was a dwarf, with the strength in his arms to handle a very heavy whip.

Fig. 4.12. End connection for twelve-horse hitch. The connection of the thong is made from a middled strand, each side of which is split in two and the four parts braided over the end of the thong and knotted. It is set on a notch in the handle as a swivel sling.

Fig. 4.13. Solid leather thong. This whip was made by Elmer Seybold. This thong is formed of two pieces of cowhide sewn together, tapered and rounded. The sling string is tied on as a separate piece, as is the fall. The thong is eight feet long, about the maximum length that can be cut on the length of a side of leather, the fall twenty-one inches. The handle is nineteen inches long, hand-shaved hickory. This type of thong could be made by saddlers who did not braid, but had both the leather and the sewing machines. This whip does not crack well, but could be used for touching up a horse.

with the whip on his right shoulder, stock on front, thong trailing behind. The bullwhackers used both hands and threw their whips sideways, not overhand.

When the first cattle were brought from Texas to the Great Plains the drovers used a whip with a wood handle and a separate thong, much like the shorter-handled muleskinner's whip or Florida Cow whip. This style of whip is seen in the paintings of Charles Russell, often draped around the neck of the horseman.

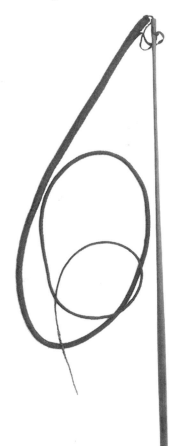

Fig. 4.14. Bullock whip. This bullock whip was made by Elmer Seybold in about 1927. It was made for a Smackover Slim, a bullock driver from Smackover, Arizona, who met with an accident before picking it up. It has a 6 ½-foot handle and a 12-foot thong with a braided seagrass popper. The thong is about 1 ½ inches in diameter at the heavy end. It is heavily loaded, the core being a rubber gas hose with musket (32 calibre) balls inside.

Fig. 4.15. Bullock whip, connection of thong to handle. The connection of the thong is made with a separate strand passing through the end of the thong and around it, middled, with the two ends through an axial hole in the end of the handle and out, one to the side, and tied. It is set on the handle as a swivel sling.

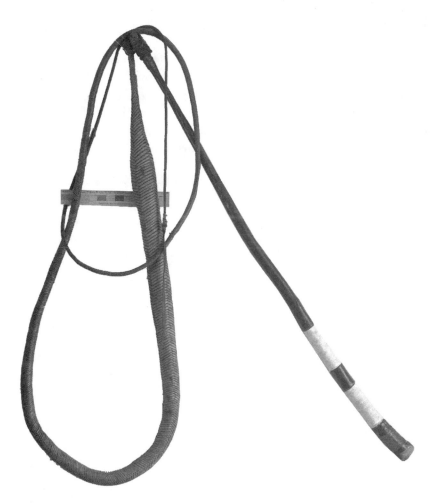

Fig. 4.16. Bullock whip. This bullock whip has been repaired at both ends. It came up for auction in England in 1965, together with an item identified as being from Wells Fargo. The handle at that time was a fancy turned wood, 14 inches long. The thong is a 20-strand rawhide braid, ¾ inch diameter at the keeper, 2.7 inch diameter at the wide point a foot from the keeper, decreasing to 1.7 inches at 4 feet, 1 inch at 7 feet, and finishing at ¼ inch at 16½ feet. This thong was probably one used by American bullwhackers taking freight across the plains. Commercial braiders would make their thongs in leather normally, but amateurs were likely to use rawhide, often readily available at no cost. Some bullwackers were known to make their own whips. Dry, this thong weighs 6 ¼ pounds. Filled with grease or wet it would be significantly heavier. The handle shown is 4½ feet long. Three- to 4-foot handles were reported to be usual for the bullwackers at the time this whip would have been used. Courtesy K.J. Lewis.

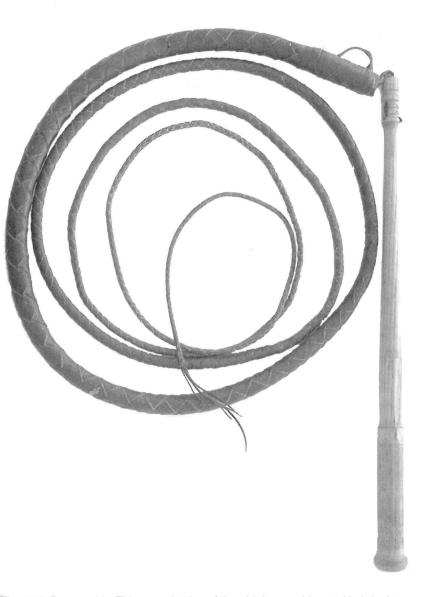

Fig. 4.17. Drover whip. This reproduction of the old drover whip used in bringing cattle to the Great Plains was made by Elmer Seybold. It is connected to the handle by a sling string that goes through an axial hole in the handle then outside and ties in place. This connection was later superseded by a swivel sling string in a notch in the end of the handle. The handle is nineteen inches long. The thong ends in an unfinished kangaroo point.

Chapter 5
Machine Braiding - Diamond Whip Co.

When cattle replaced buffalo on the short-grass prairie of the western plains, the need for cattle whips and heavier whips for transportation expanded greatly. The Diamond Whip Company was established in Chicago in 1878 to take advantage of this expanded market. They stopped making whips about 1950, when the market was much reduced. G. L. Soreghen, who had owned the Diamond Whip Company when they were still producing whips, was very helpful with regard to their operation. Catalog No. 24 of the Diamond Whip Co. is reproduced in Appendix F.

The Diamond Whip Company approached the industrial production of whips in a fashion similar to the industrial revolution in New England, with all the hallmarks of the Yankee Knack. Making whips was closely organized as a volume process. Using leather, a material of great variety, variability, and multiple uses, the company organized a wide range of braided products and associated leather products in a balanced fashion, developed specialized machines and equipment to minimize labor cost, and tanned their own leather. Ultimately the sets for the thongs were cut by machine and braided by machines. Some hand finishing was necessary, but this was held to a minimum.

The Diamond Whip Company made a full line of whips and quirts. Situated in Chicago, they were at the transportation hub to the expanding cattle regions of the far west and the farming regions of the long-grass prairie. They carried regional styles to suit all users, but cattle whips were the main product. Cattle whips of the bullwhip style were used extensively in moving cattle through the stockyards, which may have accounted for a large proportion of bullwhips sold by Diamond Whip. They sold only to jobbers, rather than direct to dealers. Jobbers took whips by the gross, while dealers only wanted a few whips. Selling to jobbers reduced their sales costs, but because of the markup needed by the jobbers, pricing had to be low to compete against individual whipmakers or saddleries who sold direct to dealers.

Tanning their own hides offered the Diamond Whip Company two advantages: they were in control of quality and could produce and use full hides, rather than the sides that were common on the market. The tannery was a significant part of the organization and provided the full range of tannages required, including an alum-tanned split cowhide, rather than an Indian-tanned buck, that they used as buckskin. An individual craftsman would find it costly to use a similar wide range of leather, and even a whipmaker working for a saddlery would not have the full range available to him. The whipmakers working for a saddlery also might be called on to use up sides that had turned out to be unsuitable for other uses and might not be entirely suitable for whips.

Sets of strands for whip thongs were cut from the hides on a table with circular knives. The strands were cut at a slant, so that the grain surface covered the entire surface of the braid and the strands were tapered to suit the thong. The strands were cut full length (twice the length of the finished whip), and in six-strand whips, strands were not dropped as the diameter of the whip became smaller. Cutting was by hand initially, but in time they were cut by machine. I did not learn whether the hides were cut in precise circles or just around the hide, whether a gang cutter was used to cut several strands at a time or just a single cutter, if the machine-cut strands were guided by hand. There is an obvious economy in using the hide if the cutting can follow the outline of the hide, rather than a strict circle cut from the hide. The sets were all cut to a yoke at the heavy end of the whip, which was the start of the braid.

The factory had five braiding machines and everything was braided by machine when the machine operation was fully developed. The braiding machines were not the flat-bed type, with the racers or bobbins running in a flat plane, as used with thread in covering buggy whips', but a bowl type, with the racers running inside a round bowl. Thongs were braided from the butt to the

Fig. 5.1. Bowl-style braiding machine. This bowl-style braiding machine was used to braid leather, as whips, reins or halters, or braided leather grips on buggy whips.

Fig. 5.2. Interior of bowl-style braiding machine. The racers on the inside of the bowl-style machine held the leather strands to be braided. They were driven around their path by the gearing on the outside of the machine.

Whips of the West

point. The tension on the strands was twenty-five to thirty-five pounds, too much for a hand braider to maintain for long. To prepare the strands for braiding, they were soaked in an emulsion of neutral soap. Such soaking would help the strands stretch and conform in shape during braiding, and ensure a tight, long-lasting braid.

The centers for the heavy whips were made of belting leather, from the edges cut off when making industrial pulley belts. These edges were top-quality leather, and cheap, as the alternative was to get rid of them by burning. A bundle of strands were cut to the proper taper and tied with a wet cotton cable on a roping machine. The cotton cable tightened as it dried. The edges were in plentiful supply, as Chicago was a center for tanning. A cattle whip operation by itself did not generate sufficient flank or other lower-quality leather to fill the need for bellies, and in such operations bellies might be made of rope or even paper, contributing little to the thong apart from bulk.

Fig. 5.3. Rope core for bullwhip. Cores of rope, roughly tapered, are used in some bullwhips. The rope core builds up the diameter, provides taper and some strength but little weight.

Machine Braiding—Diamond Whip Co.

Fig. 5.4. Paper Core for bullwhip. This core for a Bucheimer bullwhip is made of paper. The paper core provides a taper to the whip and builds up the diameter, but does not offer strength or weight. The whip production business has always been competitive, and once the larger discriminating market decreased, quality could be neglected in favor of cost. Bucheimer is no longer in operation.

The Diamond Whip Company was organized to have the low costs necessary to compete with individual craftsmen. Using full hides made cutting easier and more economical. In cutting from a side, rather than a full hide, the strands have to be cut around a tighter circle toward the neck end, and the strands cut first along the back and then the belly will be less uniform than strands cut around the outside. Individuals might economize on leather by cutting at a steep slant and braiding so that much of the inside of the strand was on the surface. This produced a lower quality than that of the Diamond Whip Company, which cut so that the entire surface of the braid showed the grain side, the strongest part of the leather. Individuals could cut wider strands for the end of the thong, so that they could drop strands toward the end and save braiding time. Diamond Whip Company, using braiding machines, braided full length in six strands in their six-plait thongs, which was not only a good selling point, but also was easier to do on a braiding machine than to drop strands. Braiding on machines had a major advantage over braiding by hand, in that the tension

Whips of the West

Fig. 5.5. Bullwhip dropped strand. This bullwhip has the strands cut at a flat angle, leaving less grain showing on the surface of the braid. This type of cut reduced the amount of hide needed to make the overlay of the whip. The grip on the handle was wrapped with a strip of hide, which is cheaper than a braided or sewn cover. The braid starts at eight strands, goes to six, then to four at the end. The whip would be less expensive to make by hand braiding, and would be less durable than some, but would still handle well.

Machine Braiding—Diamond Whip Co.

Fig. 5.6. Bullwhip, white-hide point. This bullwhip from the 1940s has a white-hide point and had a very wide fall or slapper. The wide falls were customary for the heavy American bullwhips. It was reportedly used by Lash Larue. Courtesy R. Brown.

was both greater and constant, so the whips were more uniform in appearance. The Diamond Whip Company also had competition from prisoners in the penitentiaries. J. C. Bardell Company distributed whips made in the Moundsville Penitentiary in Virginia, until it became illegal to send work made in penitentiaries across state lines.

Bullwhip thongs could be attached to longer wood handles by tacking the yoke of the set to the wood. This attachment did not allow the thong to swivel on the handle. Alternatively, the yoke of the set for the thong could be reversed and butted against the back of the knob of the handle. It would be sewn or laced to hold it around the wood and the braiding started immediate to the knob. A knot was later put over the connection to ensure stability. A similar arrangement could be made to form a swivel keeper on steel handles. An easier, but less enduring connection, was to lash a rela-

Fig. 5.7. Wood handle. Wood handles for swivel bullwhips were turned from hickory. A thong could be attached to the longer handle either by tying the yoke around it, as shown in Fig. 5.11, or by reversing a short yoke and securing it, as shown in Fig. 5.9. Thongs were attached to the shorter handle by a short reversed yoke. The longer handle could also be used for non-swivel whips by tacking the thong in place.

Fig. 5.8. Wood handle and spike used by the Diamond Whip Company. This wood handle was used by the Diamond Whip Company for their wood-handled bull whips. The thong could be tied on at the yoke held with a reversed yoke for swiveling, or could be tacked on for a non-swivel whip. The eight-inch spike was used in whips with no separate handle to supply weight to the handle as well as stiffen the hand part.

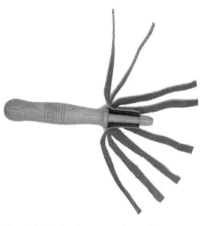

Fig. 5.9. Swivel connection of thong to wood handle. The method of connecting a thong to a wood handle using a short reversed yoke is shown here. The yoke butts up against the knob on the end of the handle. The yoke is then sewn around the wood, and the braiding can be started before the end of the handle.

Fig. 5.10. Swivel keeper on wood handle. A keeper is cut with two short sections that can butt up against the knob of the wood handle. The two sections are then sewn together to form the keeper, and a knot tied over the keeper behind the knot to keep it in place where it butts up against the knob. Larger knots than that shown were usual.

Fig. 5.11. Alternative swivel connection to wood handle. The thong on this whip is tied on to a wood handle that has a knob on the end, allowing it to swivel. The thong is cut from a yoke, starts at six strands and drops to four. The tying on the handle and the fall have both been renewed. The handle is eleven inches long.

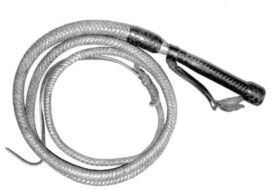

Fig. 5.12. Swivel handle bullwhip. This swivel handle bullwhip by Wyeth Hardware and Manufacturing Co. has a patented revolving iron handle. The grip has a sewn leather cover. The fall appears to have been replaced with and Australian type fall. Courtesy Fred McGehee.

Fig. 5.13. Bullwhip detail. In this detailed illustration the rawhide string that holds the thong on the swivel head of the revolving iron handle is shown. This connection made a smooth connection to the thong. Courtesy Fred McGehee.

tively wide yoke on the handle, covering the knob. Metal handles initially were very simple—a bolt going through a piece of pipe, often with a nut on it. Later, swivel handles were developed with a rotating metal knob with a hole, through which a strand of rawhide or leather could be run to anchor the thong.

Handles were not specially loaded for balance. Wood handles were not loaded at all. When a spike was used in the butt as a butt stiffener, no additional loading was added. The metal swivel handles were relatively heavy, giving the whips good balance, which would account for performers who used swivel handle bullwhips, but taped the handles so they would not swivel.

Solid leather parts, as shot bags (covers for shot or wagon whips) were cut out on clickers, which were presses with shaped knives, much like a cookie cutter. Early covers were hand laced, with the holes for the lacing punched as the cover was cut out, but later these were all sewn by machine. Solid leather team whips, wagon whips, and rawhide center express whips were made with either leather or braided covers. Individual craftsmen would not have the volume necessary to justify cutting the covers with a clicker or punching the holes for lacing. The shot-loaded team whips were made in a range of weights, up to thirty-two ounces of lead. Diamond Whip did not have so large an advantage over saddlers or others in making whips with sewn covers, as they did in making fully braided whips. Finally, all whips were rolled in a rolling machine on a glossy stone block and finished with a coating of shellac. Rawhide whips were oiled before shipment.

Cattle whips were made in a wide variety, of leather, length, and plait. They might be shot loaded or not, with a revolving handle of metal or wood, a fixed wood handle or a butt stiffened with a spike. Some whips were made with interlacing at the butt, which reinforced the first section of the thong. The whips might be braided through to the point with the leather used for the body of the whip, or the point could be made of buckskin. Individual craftsmen cutting from sides of leather might find the cutting more economical if they used buck points, in that for shorter whips they could cut the length of the side for the main part and then go to buckskin for the point. In more recent times, a white cowhide has been used for points instead of buckskin. Team or wagon whips

Fig. 5.14. Texas bullwhip. This swivel-handle bullwhip is braided from the point, Texas style. It has a double overlay in the butt section going over the strands in one direction but not in the other direction. Courtesy R. J. Greenwood.

Fig. 5.15. Texas bullwhip. The strands in the butt section of this whip are doubled in one direction, not in the other. With different color overlay this gave a variation in the pattern of the whip. Courtesy R. J. Greenwood.

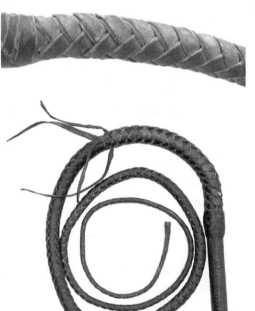

Fig. 5.16. Bullwhip. This swivel bullwhip has an overlay in the braid at the butt end. The overlay was not put onto all strands in the braid. With a different color overlay the pattern could be varied in this manner. The overlay both strengthened and increased the weight of the butt section.

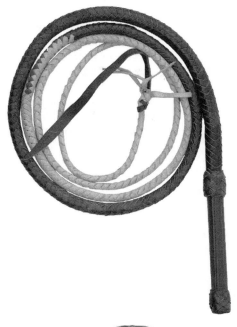

Fig. 5.17. Bucheimer bullwhip. This is a twelve-plait bullwhip made by Bucheimer with a white-hide point. A long white-hide point permits the strands for the main section of the whip to be cut along the length of the side of leather.

Fig. 5.18. Inexpensive bullwhip. This non-swivel bullwhip is braided in four strands, and has a rope core. The grip is wrapped with leather. This is a light-weight commercially made whip.

Fig. 5.19. Non-swivel wood handle bullwhip. A nicely made non-swivel bullwhip. The original fall has been replaced with a narrower Australian fall. The grip is covered with stitched leather. This whip is braided from the point, Texas style, with a heavy butt section tapering well to the point.

Fig. 5.20. Swivel-handle bullwhip. This swivel bullwhip has a composition handle. This handle was cheaper to make, as it did not require a leather covering as did an iron pipe. It did not however supply the weight to the butt end that was a big asset of the iron handle whips. This whip has a rather crude repair to the point of the whip.

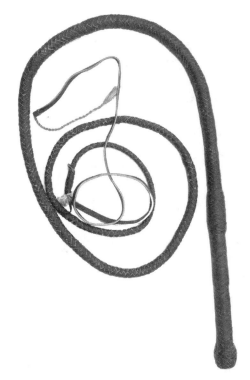

Fig. 5.21. Cable-center bullwhip. This whip has a speedometer cable in the core. It was made for use in the stockyards. Cable-center bullwhips were made by amateurs usually, rather than by the commercial whipmakers, who preferred shot loading. The cable center makes a heavy whip to handle, that falls very heavily.

were made with a solid leather core, rawhide core (as express whips), or a shot-loaded core, (as snake whips), and could be fully braided or have a partial leather cover, with a braided point of buckskin or horsehide.

Separate lashes were offered for stagecoach and horse whips. They were either California style, a lash with a straight taper from a keeper at the butt end to the point, or Texas style, with a swell belly and sling string for attaching it to a stock. A mixed California-Texas style with a straight taper and sling string was also offered. The finest buckskin lashes were all California style, up to twelve plait. The very heavy lashes for ox whips had rope cores. Diamond Whip Company did not offer whip stocks. These were available from dealers or distributors. Some were turned from hickory, but the better ones were hand shaved. A hand-shaved stock followed the grain of the wood well and did not tend to break by splitting along the grain. Some stagecoach drivers would refine the hickory whip stock by scraping it down with a piece of glass.

Chapter 6
Snake (Shot) Whips - Main and Winchester

Main & Winchester of San Francisco were large manufacturers of saddles and saddlery in the West. They supplied a wide range of whips and quirts, and claimed to be the leaders and originators in braided work. They braided entirely by hand. A comparison of Main & Winchester with the Diamond Whip Company shows the competitive nature of the trade, and niches where hand braiding could compete with a fully mechanized operation. Main & Winchester dealt directly with the dealers, rather than with jobbers or distributors, as did Diamond Whip. This not only gave them an advantage on price, but also put them in much closer contact with their dealers, allowing them to handle special orders and repairs. Appendix E shows pertinent pages of a Main & Winchester catalog from the late 1800s or early 1900s. Main & Winchester did their own tanning, an advantage in manufacturing saddles and making braided goods. Their buckskin, used extensively in both points for whips and stitching solid covers on snake whips, was from oil-tanned California deerskins. This leather would be expected to be stronger than the alum-tanned split cowhide used by Diamond Whip. This difference in buck was well known within the trade. They made a strong point that all the covers on their snake whips were buck stitched by hand, rather than machine sewn.

Main & Winchester made a wide range of snake whips, a preferred whip in the West, claiming to have made these since the California Gold Rush of 1849, and that they were in closer touch with the users than the eastern manufacturers. They used braided or twisted buck points. The snakes were offered in a range of weights up to four pounds. Some small diameter snakes were loaded with flattened bullets. This made a more dense load, but required more hand labor. Butts were wire wound on most snakes, again a labor-intensive operation. Main & Winchester appeared to have avoided much direct competition with a fully mechanized operation, such as Diamond Whip, by adding features requiring hand work. Their dog whips had an even greater diversity in work, including rope laid lashes, chain braids, crown braids, and twisted handles, all restricted to hand work. Since dog whips are short, the benefits of machine braiding were reduced because of the set-up time, so a hand braiding operation could more easily compete even without the special braids.

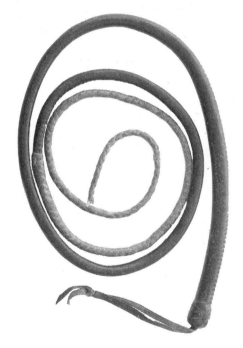

Fig. 6.1. Snake whip. A relatively well-preserved snake whip, with original buckskin point and wrist loop.

Fig. 6.2. Snake whip, repaired. This heavy snake whip has had the point renewed and a wrist loop attached. These heavy whips allowed a lot of stress to be put on the point of the whip if they were used with a hard throw.

Fig. 6.3. Snake whip. This snake is sewn with two threads. Most were sewn or buckstitched with one thread in an over-and-over pattern. The braided buckskin point appears to be original.

Whips of the Wes

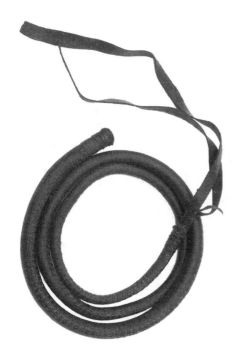

Fig. 6.4. Pocket snake whip. This pocket snake has seen hard use. The knob at the butt is gone, although the wire winding remains. The point has been replaced with a double fall of thin wide leather. Farmers who hired crews to harvest their hay often would insist that the men use double falls on their whips so that their horses or mules would not be abused or cut up by whips.

Main & Winchester offered a full range of California-style coach and team lashes, in buck and in horsehide with buck points. They emphasized the quality of the buck and the hand braiding, although it is difficult to imagine that a sixteen-plait sixteen-foot stagecoach lash could be hand braided competitively with one braided by machine.

Main & Winchester offered a very limited range of drover or cattle whips. Here they supplied a range of plaits and lengths, which would be relatively easy to organize within a hand-braiding operation. They also offered an Australian-American style with the lash on a looped swivel handle, again a style requiring more hand work. It is apparent that they did not attempt to compete head on with the machine braided drover or bullwhips, where the machine braided whips had such a strong advantage. They appear more to have wanted to offer some variety in whips to their dealers.

Fig. 6.5. Coach thong. This is a finely plaited buckskin coach lash. These lashes were made in four plait to sixteen plait, four feet to sixteen feet long, in both a light weight for stage coach use and a heavier weight for use with teams. They were usually bull necked, i.e., a straight taper from butt to end, but some had a swell belly. The better lashes were braided over a buckskin core, but lower qualities might have a core of other leather.

Fig. 6.6. Coach thong cracker. The cracker on a coach lash was thread braided into the end of the lash. In this cracker, the buckskin from the core of the lash continues on as a core for the cracker. The crackers wear out before the lash normally. Main & Winchester made a point of being willing to replace worn crackers.

Whips of the West

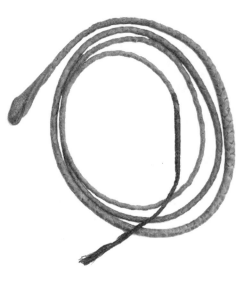

Fig. 6.7. Swell-belly coach thong. This is a swell-belly coach thong, four-strand braid in buckskin. A straight taper was generally preferred for coach and team thongs, but swell-belly thongs were available. Courtesy Ellis V. Horn.

Fig. 6.8. Linen thong. Linen lashes for coach whips or team whips could be braided over a leather core by machine. They provided a cheaper but less robust thong than one braided of buckskin or horse hide. Courtesy Ellis V. Horn.

Chapter 7
Regional and Local Whipmakers

In a fashion similar to that of Main & Winchester, small or independent whipmakers could find a niche, either selling to dealers, or more often to the ultimate user. They could offer custom work or unique styles. Amateur and part-time workers, such as cowboys braiding whips in the off-season, might work very cheaply, undercutting everyone else on price. Cowboys often were able to get rawhide free, and much of their braiding was done in rawhide, probably in part because of this cost advantage. Tom Hill of Australia, compared the amateur whipmaker to a pimple on the rear end of the professional whipmaker.

Regional influences on the whips used in the West were from Texas, Florida, and Australia by way of California,. Texas whips were fundamentally Mongol whips, braided from the point, lacking good taper, often with a swell belly to compensate for the lack of taper. The lashes were normally attached to the handle with a sling string. Texas bullwhips were braided from the point, had a lack of taper in the main section to the point, and usually were heavy near the butt. They were tacked to a wooden handle which might be relatively long compared with other bullwhips. Mexican whips were taken to Hawaii when the first cattle ranches were established there. Some whips were made in a mixed Australian-American style, with a short handle and a heavy thong. The California whips had a keeper attachment to the handle, as did the whips from the northeastern states and English whips, and a straight taper from the butt. The Florida cow whip is a Mongol style whip formerly lacking a good taper, attached to a wood handle by a sling string.

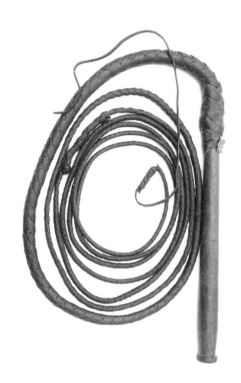

Fig. 7.1. Show whip, Texas style. This whip was put together from two Texas bullwhips. The handle is twenty inches long. The thong is heavy at the butt end but rapidly decreases in diameter with a long, thin point. Tied to this was a second long thin point from another whip. John Mc Nish, who showed as Dakota Jack, used this whip to throw letters on the floor, as a variant on the trick usually thought of as being done with a rope.

Fig. 7.2. Hawaiian stock whip. Mexican vaqueros came to Hawaii when the first cattle operations were established at the Parker Ranch there in 1847. This whip was made by a Japanese-Hawaiian named Nikata, whose grandfather had learned from the Mexicans. The handle is koa wood. The thong is rawhide, braided from the point Mexican style. The traditional style has been closely maintained. Courtesy Alex Green.

Fig. 7.3. Hawaiian bullwhip. This bullwhip was copied from the American whips about 1900. This is again made by Nikata, who makes both stockwhips and bullwhips for the paniolos, the Hawaiian cattlemen, to suit their personal choice. Courtesy Alex Green.

Fig. 7.4. Austral-American whip. This is a whip known as an Austral-American whip. It has a fairly heavy eight-inch handle with a keeper directly connected to the keeper on the rawhide thong. The heavy handle gives the whip a nice balance. It does not swivel. A partially obliterated notice on the handle suggested it was patented July 7, 1903. The general appearance suggests it was made by Wyeth Hardware and Manufacturing Company, who later made a similar whip with a swivel handle. Diamond Whip Company and Main & Winchester also made this style of whip.

Whips of the West

Fig. 7.5. Pocket snake whip. This pocket snake has a tail of twisted latigo. The tail is in two sections, allowing the end to be replaced readily. The butt is wire wound. The body of the whip is lead shot with a solid leather sewn cover. Pocket snakes with sewn covers did not stand up well, since the heavy load and small diameter lead to high stress in the cover during use.

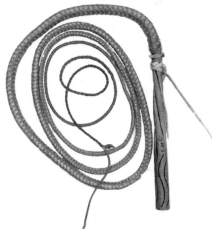

Fig. 7.6. Florida drover whip. This two-tone drover whip was made by Claude Sheppard. It has a twisted point and a wear leather between the thong and the handle. The handle is hand carved. The better handles were usually carved, rather than turned.

The Florida drover (or cow) whip was made widely by independent whipmakers, and showed variations in style. The handle is short, about thirteen inches long, turned or hand carved, with a thong usually ten to twelve feet long. The thong is attached to the handle by a double leather sling string going through a hole in the end of the handle and coming out to the side. There is usually a wear leather against the end of the handle. The last two to three feet of the thong are usually twisted rather than braided, with a nylon or other cracker on the end. The thong may be bull necked in shape, with a moderate taper, or sometimes snake shaped or frog belly, i.e., the snake that has swallowed a frog. Early whips had very little taper, if any, but are now tapered reasonably well. The preferred leather was deerskin, but goat or calf could be used for the main section. Indian-tanned buckskin was very much preferred for the twisted end.

I have found nothing recorded on the making of the Florida Cow whip, or Spanish Drover whip, as it is also called. Claude Sheppard of Gainesville, Florida, provided me with extensive samples and background information on this whip. The whip was not commonly used in the West, although it had some influence on the drover whip used early on in bringing the cattle up from Texas to the plains.

According to Mr. Sheppard, the Florida Cow whip was brought to America from Spain when the Spanish settled in Florida. The earliest were Mongol-type whips with very little taper, on a short fourteen to sixteen inch handle, about thongs twenty to thirty feet long. They were used from the ground with cattle run in open country. After the Spanish lost control of Florida, the whips were made locally, and have been made by users or independent whip-makers ever since. In 1976, when Mr. Sheppard discussed these whips, there were still a few seventeen- to eighteen-foot whips being used in grassy pastures, but most were about twelve feet long, used mainly from horseback.

Claude Sheppard cut the strands by first cutting a wide strip backward and forward on the skin. The strip was stretched out and anchored at one end, and the strands cut from it using the thumbnail as a guide. He had tried cutting around the skin, but didn't like that method. Deerskin is soft and stretchy, and it would be easier to cut narrow strands from a prestretched strip. He apparently was not familiar with cutting strands by drawing them through a gang of knives, which works well with buckskin.

The core of the thong was about two-thirds braided, one-third twisted. A twelve-foot thong would have six-foot core. The twisted end was Indian-tanned buckskin. The strands were spliced either in the usual fashion of burying them inside the braid and then bringing them to the outside, or by overlapping them with the strands in the braid. The two pairs of strands running in opposite spirals were put together flesh side to flesh side and twisted.

John Schoewe was producing Florida Cow whips in the early 1960s. He had spent some time with Cecil Henderson in Australia in 1942, and learned Australian techniques. He produced mainly stock

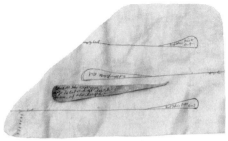

Fig. 7.7. Deerskin with strip laid out for cutting. This piece of deerskin is laid out for cutting into a strip that will be cut into the strands for a drover whip. The average width of the piece cut out at the turn at its wide end was about 1 ¼ inch.

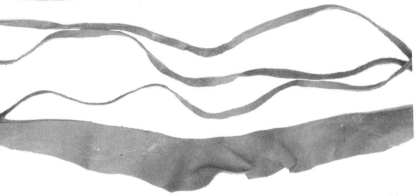

Fig. 7.8. Cutting strands from the strip. The strip of deerskin as cut from the skin was about 2 ½ inches wide. This was stretched and then cut into eight strands. These strands would then stretch sufficiently to form a smooth braid. The end of the strip was held in a vice, and the strands cut using the thumb as a guide.

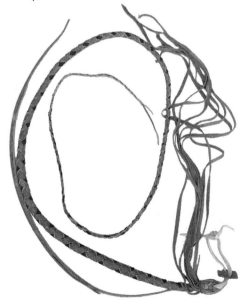

Fig. 7.9. Demonstration belly for Florida drover whip. This figure shows a belly for a Florida drover whip as made by Claude Sheppard. The completed belly is shown with the strands for the overlay tied in place. An extra solid hide section to shape the swell belly, which is in the core of the belly, is shown alongside the belly. This core is six feet long, suitable for a twelve- or thirteen-foot whip. The swell belly insert starts at the butt end of the thong, reaches its maximum diameter at about a foot, and finishes at about thirty inches.

Regional and Local Whipmakers

Fig. 7.10. Florida drover whip detail. This shows the detail of how the strands for the overlay are tied onto the belly at the start.

Fig. 7.11. Demonstration end of Florida drover whip. This shows an alternative style of putting the strand on the thong that attaches to the handle. The strand is put through the end of the braid from the center to the outside, wrapped around one and a half times, then back inside and out the end, where the two ends of the strand are tied together leaving two long ends to attach to the handle. This style of attachment was more often used in times past.

Fig. 7.12. Tying on the strands for twisting. The strands to form the twisted point could be either started inside the core of the braid or tied onto the strands of the braid and braided with them for a distance. Claude Sheppard preferred the latter method.

Fig. 7.13. Florida drover whip handle. This is an old-style spool handle, hand carved. It is fourteen inches long. The axial hole in the end extends out to both sides.

whips, and supplied the whip performers of the time. His work was very good (Schultz 1965). John Schoewe made the cow whip in kangaroo with buckskin ends. His whips were well tapered, and his whips may have inspired others in Florida to put more taper into their whips. Although the cow whips tended toward having more taper in later years, the method for using them to crack continued to be that of throwing them out in a strong overhand throw and then jerking them back sharply, as was required for a whip with no taper.

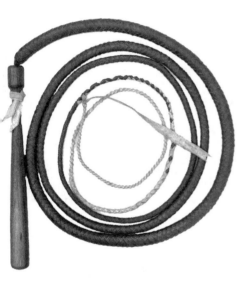

Fig. 7.14. Florida drover whip by John Schoewe. John Schoewe was an outstanding American whipmaker. He spent some time with Cecil Henderson when in Australia in 1942 during World War II, and later made whips for performers and the cattlemen in Florida. His Florida drover whips were well tapered and probably contributed much to the improvement in taper of these whips as made by others. He tanned his own buckskin for the points. He did not use a wear leather between thong and handle.

Nowadays most Florida Cow whips are made of nylon, usually loaded to give them some weight. These whips have the advantage that they do not rot in the hot humid Florida climate as leather whips do. They are strong and can be used to heel rope young calves. In recent years some whips have been sold in the West to ranchers who found them convenient to tie onto their saddles However, they are no substitute for an Australian stock whip in working cattle.

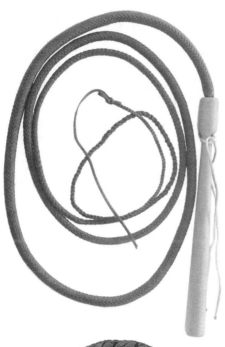

Fig. 7.15. Florida nylon drover whip. This Florida drover whip was made by Krist King in nylon parachute cord. These whips stand up well to the warm damp climate and will take a lot of abuse. The handle is sixteen inches long.

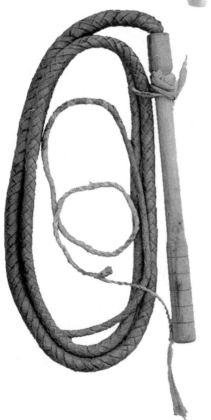

Fig. 7.16. Florida deerskin drover whip. This whip was made by Krist King. It has a deerskin thong with a separate twisted point. The handle is sixteen inches long. King did not normally taper the strands for his whips, hence the need for a separate twisted point.

A regional whip was developed in California in the cattle country east of Sacramento from the coach thong. Cowboys either got thongs from a woman near Folsom who braided coach thongs or learned from her how to make them. They attached the thongs to a handle shaved down from the spoke of a wagon wheel. As developed, these whips were made of buckskin, ten feet long braided to a buckskin popper, and lightly loaded the first eighteen inches from the butt end. They were mounted on a handle usually made from a wagon spoke, eighteen to twenty-four inches long, shaved down to flex well. The thong was attached by a sling string in a notch at the end of the handle. They were very fast, light whips. T. M. Kerr of Clements, California who provided background on these whips, made some and repaired many, as horses stepped on the end. I traded him an Australian stockwhip for one of his, and after that he started putting an Australian-type fall on the whip, making it much simpler to maintain.

Fig. 7.17. California cattle whip. This whip was made by Tom Kerr. The handle is twenty-three inches long. This whip is more fancy than the usual, with a hand grip and a cover over the sling string. The body of the whip is braided from cowhide with the core loaded over the first eighteen inches. The point is buckskin. When Indian tanned buckskin was more readily available the entire braid would have been buckskin. This is a very fast whip.

Another whip was being made in the 1950s in this region by Pete Tabeau. He apparently had been a stagecoach driver, and made whips when he was older. His whips had an eight-plait thong with the last three to four feet done in buckskin. They were mounted on a wood handle, connected with a double loop, the loop on the handle able to swivel. He sold directly to users, and made them from very heavy to light as desired. Similar whips of this type were also made entirely in latigo leather, braided from the point Mexican style.

Australian stock whips are well known and sometimes used in parts of the West. Visiting Australian stockmen have introduced them in many areas, and some ranchers have taken them up and use them Australian style. I had a full accounting of one Canadian cowboy's use of the Australian stock whip when he came down to pick up a whip. He was working at one of the large ranches in British Columbia and had become acquainted with these whips

Fig. 7.18. Whip by Pete Tabeau. This photo is the best I could get of a whip by Pete Tabeau. Tom Kerr, who gave me information on Pete Tabeau, repaired some of his whips. Kerr tried to obtain one for me to look at, but although he knew several people who were using them, none were willing to part with their whip. This was a good indication of the quality of the work. The handles had a swivel keeper and the keepers of thong and handle were directly linked. The point of the whip was braided in buckskin to three or four feet. The body of the whip was latigo in an eight-strand braid.

Whips of the West

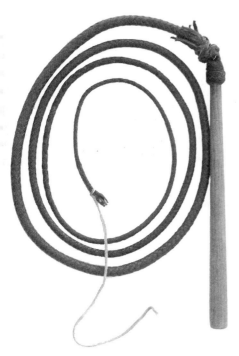

Fig. 7.19. California stock whip. This stock whip was made in California. It is similar in some ways to the whip made by Pete Lebeau. It was braided Mexican style from the point and attached directly to the swivel keeper on the handle. The strands of the braid at the butt were put through the keeper and tied into a knot. A second knot was put behind this knot, over the ends of the strands from the first knot. Taper of the whip is good.

Fig. 7.20. California stock whip thong. The splitting of the strands in the four strand section to go to eight strands can be seen in the central section in this illustration.

Fig. 7.21. California stock whip attachment detail. The detail of the connection between the thong and the swivel keeper on the handle is shown in this illustration.

from some Australians who were working at the ranch. At the time I met him he was the only one on the ranch using a stock whip They moved very large herds of cattle at this ranch. He told me that when he was riding drag, pushing the rear of a herd along, he would cover about three times the width of the herd that the cow boys without whips could cover, and that the cows tended to bell out in front of him. I enquired why the boss did not buy whips for everyone. He looked askance at this, and replied that he did it his way, and the others did it theirs. Cowboys are an independent lot When they were driving a herd along a sidehill he would ride point on the downward side. Instead of having to ride down the hill and then push the cattle up when they were moving too far down, he would crack his whip so the sound went across the valley and the echo would push the cattle up. This saved his horses a great deal He also whip-broke his horses. He would put the horse in a round pen, and approach it to calm it and allow it to get used to him. If the horse turned away, he would hit it on the rear with the whip he had been carrying behind his back. He might have to repeat this a time or two before the horse would stand facing him when ie approached. A horse so started would turn and face him if he racked his whip or even slapped his chaps. This could keep a horse out of trouble if it took off when unsaddled with the girth not fully unbuckled, as he could quickly stop the horse and get the saddle off properly.

Shot-loaded team whips were commonly used for working cattle in parts of Wyoming and Montana. The U.S. Cavalry was active in this region for many years, driving the Indians off their lands, and they appear to have used the shot-loaded team whips with the cavalry wagons. Many of these whips could have ended up in the hands of the early cowboys and established them as the whip for working cattle there. Shot whips were a common whip in the West in general. A pocket snake was made small enough to fit into a pocket. This whip was a popular whip with Hamley's of Pendleton. The pocket snakes might have a sewn cover or be braided. Various points were used on them.

Fig. 7.22. Pocket Snake. Pocket snake with wire-wound butt and kangaroo point, as supplied to Hamley's in Pendleton, Oregon.

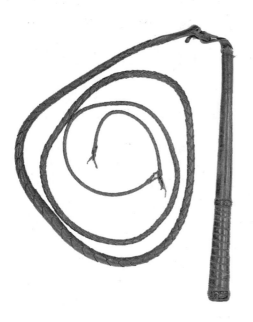

Fig. 7.23. Old American stock whip. This old stock whip has a swell-belly thong. The keeper on the handle is loose, and the thong is attached to the handle by a leather strand tying the two keepers together. This may be a matter that the owner was unfamiliar with the method of putting two keepers together with a lark's head knot. The handle has a sewn leather cover and the hand part is wound with copper wire to improve the grip. The winding is spaced to provide a grip, rather than kept together as done on snake whips to strengthen the butt. The whip may be either American made or imported.

Fig. 7.24. Old American stock whip detail. This shows the detail of the copper wire winding on the grip, with the end held in place with a leather knot. The cover for the handle was sewn inside out and then turned out putting the seam inside. The strands for the thong were not pared, although they were tapered well to suit the changing diameter of the thong.

Fig. 7.25. Old American horse quirt. This quirt is shot loaded. The shot bag is held with string. The bag broke a few inches from the butt end, where there is a lot of bending stress during use. Courtesy H. Vierling.

Fig. 7-26. Deteriorated lead shot. The lead shot in the old quirt had ground itself down to a small size and a powder as it rubbed together during use.

Fig. 7-27. Quirt belly. This older American quirt has a shot-loaded belly, wrapped with string. The end of the belly has a plug of solid leather strips about three inches long.

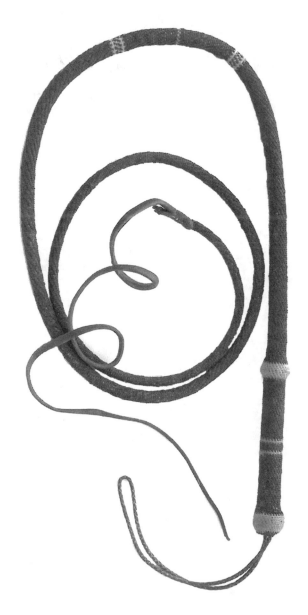

Fig. 7.28. Horsehair whip. Whips were occasionally covered with horse hair as show whips. The whip would be basically a braided leather whip, with the cover as ornament. This whip has a cover done in Spanish hitching. They were also made in the usual hitching, which made a somewhat heavier cover because of the string, but was very attractive.

Whips of the West

Appendix A
Westfield, The "Whip City," Picturesque Hampden.

Man with Whip

In the beginning you will be inclined to exclaim: "Few things are so simple as a whip!" Not many articles of commerce have so ancient a lineage, though, that can be directly traced.

Of the thousands who buy whips to sell again, of the millions who buy whips to use, few are there among them who have the simplest comprehension of the processes involved in their manufacture.

A whip looks so simple when made that it is dismissed from further thought, as merely a whip! If we go backward along the lines of the

HISTORY OF THE RACE

the record of Babylonian cylinders, Assyrian monuments, Egyptian tombs, Grecian bas-reliefs, Roman Parthenon friezes, and middle age art, all bear evidence to the use and importance of the whip in the unfolding of the life of the people of various countries.

But of whips, as of so many other things, it was left to American genius to evolve a rude, simple thing into a highly organized product, requiring capital, machinery and skilled labor to bring about the perfection of seeming simplicity of the American whip.

I say American whip advisedly, because the result of this evolution of ingenuity has been the production of a type that is purely national. What is technically known as the "bow" whip is

A RESULT OF YANKEE THOUGHT

and it is pre-eminently the whip of this country.

An Englishman, German, Spaniard, indeed, any foreigne
requires a shrub, a bit of rawhide, a knife and patience and he ca
produce a goad of one sort or another to suit his fancy or need
The more highly organized mechanical faculty of the Americar
to produce a whip to his liking, demands a whale, a ship and sai
ors to hunt it, the gut of the cat, a rattan jungle in India, a hickor
grove in his native country, a cotton plantation, mulberry trees an
silk worms, a forest of rubber trees, the hide of the buck, foss
gum from Africa, linseed oil, iron, paint, the art of the turner an
designer in metal, the tusks of the elephant, gold, silver and variou
alloys, the hoofs of animals, the product of the Ilax field, preciou
stones, the genius of the mechanic in the invention of strange an
novel machinery,

THE ACUTEST BUSINESS AND EXECUTIVE ABILITY;

then he goes to work to produce that simple article of trade—
whip!

When put upon the market it can he bought for twenty-fiv
cents, or you can run to the extremes of luxury that are represente
by hundreds of dollars, but the essential principle of manufactur
is the same in either case.

Burns wrote his immortal verse on a plain deal table; Senec
extolled the blessings of poverty, preparing his argument on a soli
gold table. The means used to produce the expression did nc
modify the genius in either case. The whip costing a dollar will las
as long, produce as stinging a blow, and be as useful an instrumen
in conveying your sentiments to the cuticle of the animal, as on
costing a hundred times as much.

It would appear, then, that the manufacture of a whip is a ver
interesting process, well worthy of investigation. Let us look into it

To do this thoroughly and understandingly it is necessary t
journey to a small town in western Massachusetts, Westfield b
name, that is

'HE CRADLE OF THE INDUSTRY,

and to-day stands forth without a rival in all the world as the vhip center.

Here we see a flourishing town, whose chief and practically vhose only industry is the making of whips.

It has no parallel that we know of in this or any country in the ivilized world.

And this great business has all been evolved in so short a time s that which elapsed between the year 1808 and the present! In this onnection we quote from a trade periodical a little of the history of he early years. It reads:

At this time (1808) there lived in Westfield a man named OSEPH JOKES, Who happened to become the owner of a choice ot of hickory. His many friends frequently called on him to be bliged with a piece of this wood for whipstocks, whips being then 1ome made. Finally Jokes made some of these stocks and offered hem for sale. A little later he conceived the idea of putting a lash n the stock. The lash consisted of a heavy strip of horsehide, which vas made fast to the stock by a 'keeper,' and thus we have the first vhip made in Westfield.

Jokes did quite a business, and

)THER MEN BEGAN IMPROVING ON THE STOCK

by boiling the wood in a preparation of oil and coloring. The ecipes for making these preparations were secrets among those vho made whips, so each one had a preparation of his own; but ome were much better than others.

Five years later lashes were made, by narrow strips of raw, 1orse or cowhide, and plaited into cords, very much the same as It present. A piece of leather, rolled round and beveled, to make he swell, was inclosed in the center. The lash was rolled between)locks, and then varnished. In 1820 the experiment of plaiting a :overing of cotton thread over the stocks was tried, hut was only)artially successful, as it was done entirely by hand, holding the tock on the knees.

At this time different materials began to be used for stocks rattan, and the best of all for the purpose, whalebone.

WHEN WHALEBONE WAS FIRST BROUGHT INTO USE

the entire stock was made of it, a thing rarely afforded at the present time. Whalebone is now used in manufacturing the drop on account of its tenacity. After some degree of completeness had been acquired in plaiting Over the stock, an attempt, with success was made to bring into use the drop whip, which, of course, wa only a combination of stock and lash, and covered the entire length thus dispensing with the 'keeper.' This was a decided improve ment, and many whips, in a small way and slow process, wer made and offered for sale.

About 1822 an invention was brought into use for whip plait ing by Hiram Hull, father of an ex-president of the American Whip Company at Westfield. Mr. Hull was the first man to start wha could well be called a factory, when this invention was used It resembled a barrel in appearance from its shape, and wa also called a barrel.

The whip to be cov-
ered was suspended
by the top, and hung
down in the Center
of the barrel. A
number of threads
were attached to the
top of the whip, and
hung over the edge
of the barrel, with
weights to keep them
in position. These
weights Were worked
by the hand, throw-
ing them in opposite
directions, thus

The Automatic Bounder.

PLAITING THE WHIP

almost as perfectly as at the present time, though the process was a very slow one. This invention Was in use through a number

Whips of the West

The Old Fashioned Plaiting Machine.

of years, and an expert at working it was looked upon as a good tradesman. Women are said to have attained quite a speed in working the threads with their nimble fingers. The process is shown in the engraving entitled 'The old-fashioned plaiting machine.'

The plaiting of to-day is made on the same principle as the one just described.

The drop whip passed through quite a number of years unmolested; then the drop began to decrease, and finally a whip was made perfectly straight, and took the name of the bow, or the trotting whip; thus the three kinds of whips were in use that are now, viz. Whips with lash and keeper, drop whips, and bow or trotters' whips.

Adapted from "Harness" (trade magazine), New York. Engravings made expressly for this work.

In 1855, a self-plaiting machine turned by a crank, came into use by American design and ingenuity. This improvement tended to increase the Whip industry about a third in five years, and during the next semi-decade this invention was largely improved upon, and in 865 Westfield produced about one-half a million dollars' worth of whips. Trade in whips largely increased, companies were formed, and a year later statistics showed that

The Rolling Machine.

WESTFIELD LED THE WORLD

in the extent of her whip industry.

So great has been the advance in the value of the product tha what stood for the sum of it in 1865, does not now serve to repre sent the sales of more than one factory!

Hiram Hull, spoken of in the quotation above, is practically th inventor of scientific whip making, as he was the founder of th American Whip Company, which under his guidance pioneere the industry and later, through the energy and tact of Ira Miller, it present chief officer, has assumed a leading position, with the enor mous output of over two million five hundred thousand whips pe annum!

As the experiments, trials and successes of Mr. Hull were actu ally a part of the history of the American Whip Company, under th various firm and corporate names, it is fitting that we take this grea factory as typical of the growth of whip making, and in detailing it progress and methods of manufacture we shall really be

The Whalebone Rack.

GOING TO THE FOUNTAIN HEAD FOR FACTS.

The process I shal describe will be confinec to the "bow" or straigh whip, because it is typical although the Americar Whip Company makes a great variety of all mer chantable styles of whips. The bow whip is sim plicity itself. It is composec of what is technically knowr as the "stock" and a "snap," but the processes that are gone through to produce this simplicity are really quite intricate.

Entering the office of the American Whip Company, I first note at the clerical force in the office department does not seem to e numerous. Here is the first evidence of a carefully evolved system that grows on one as he proceeds. No superfluous persons old down office stools; no unnecessary employe's stand around to ock progress. For convenience I will suppose I am

N ORDER FOR ONE HUNDRED DOZEN

of whips, and will go through the factory, much as such an rder would go, skipping now and then some details, for the sake f brevity and continuity of narrative.

The order tag never skips, as you may judge when I tell you that is tag is handled some one hundred and fifty times before it is led on the completion of the order.

When the tag is duly filled in with the particulars of the order, he first step is in the direction of the rattan house. This is a storage uilding situated to one side of the main factory, in which is stored housands of dollars' worth Singapore rattan. It is unassorted just s it has arrived from the vessel that landed it in New York. It is one han's duty to select it, grade it and pass it on into the works. This eems simple, but it is a work of nice discrimination, perfection in only being acquired by long practice in handling the bundles.

Meantime, in a large room, that is the basement of the front build-hg of the works, are men employed selecting the whalebone, which

s here stored in bun-les in racks that look ke nothing so much as he pigeonhole contriv-nce they have in hotel oat rooms for stow-hg away one's bag-age. The contents of hese racks, however, hount to thousands of ollars in value.

Braiding Leather Lashes.

AA POUND OF WHALEBONE

does not amount to much in hulk; neither does a ten-dollar bi
which is its equivalent.

The bone, as it is called, is not as straight as the narrow patl
at first, but it must be made so before it can become fitted to its us
This is where you come into contact with the first expert. Men tak
the slender wands, and by careful manipulation, using heat, sanc
paper and patience, finally square, round, taper and point the bon
until its condition is perfect for whip purposes.

Some of the whips in my order call for hide "centers." The ra
hide is twisted into long, thin sticks that in form resemble the bon
When dry it is sandpapered and polished and pointed with tl
same care and accuracy as the bone.

The center, I should perhaps explain, is that part of the stoc
that extends upward, making the tip end. It gives the flexibility an
snap that a good whip possesses. The depth of these centers varie
A "full bone" whip has a whale bone center extending nearly c
quite to the butt end, or handle. A quarter bone, of course, does nc
go down so deep;

THE PRICE GOVERNS THAT.

While they are Working away at these "centers," the rattan i
another section of the works, has gotten into trouble. The man wh
selected it and passed it on from the storehouse, merely took o
the rough edge, so to speak, in his work, careful as it was. Passin
into other expert hands, it is reassorted as to size, length and qua
ity, and then for the first time gets really down to business. It is pt
through machines that split it accurately into triangular pieces tha
are called "wedges," and into other pieces named "sidings." A stic
of rattan is not of large diameter, as you know, hut these machine
cut it as perfectly as if it were as large as a saw log.

At this initial stage of the proceedings the "stock" begins t
evolve. It is a sort of natural selection process. These wedges an
sidings are assembled in a particular manner so as to form a lon
stick with a merely nominal taper at one end. They form this stick i
a manner that gives it strength. An iron spike is inserted in the hick
ory "butt," a part that becomes the handle of the whip. This spik
stays just where it is placed, during the whole performance, and i

the weight producer, without which theirs would be no balance or proper "feel" to the whip. There is interesting on account of its ingenuity, around whizz the sticks and on coils the rope with a tightness of grip that would give points to a boa constrictor. In this rope they remain until dry. A little matter of a barrel of glue a day is required for this work, while two hundred and fifty tons of rope a year is alone sufficient for the winding act. But, then, five thousand pounds of rattan a day are served up to feed the maw of this voracious glue tank! Great, isn't it?

These "stocks" are a very rough, gummy looking lot of sticks when the rope is unwound and it is now requisite that they he smoothed. This is done in a turning lathe. They emerge looking quite fine, but they have got to be woven about, later on, with threads of many colors, so the surface must be nearer like polished metal. In they go the second time, into a "rounder." It Would make the whip cost too much to have a nurse follow it through all the stages of

Whip.

Office of the American Whip Company.

ts infancy, so a Whip genius invented for the American Whip Company an automatic "rounder." An armful of these sticks are tood up within reach of the "rounder," a belt is shifted on, the man goes away and

THE "ROUNDER" DOES THE REST.

The "stock" is now ready to go up stairs. It is smoothed, it has its appointed quantity of whalebone or rawhide, and it now requires a suitable covering.

This is given it by the plaiting machine. It would be as useless to attempt description of this intricate mechanism as to try to skate in July. Moreover, any one attempting to explain the machine room would rupture the larynx. It is as noisy as a political primary in a tough ward. But the work is beautiful!

Again the whip gets a rounding and a polishing until the thread covering becomes as smooth as glass and

AS HARD AS THE WESTMINISTER CATECHISM.

It passes through a number of manipulations to secure these qualities. But it is not glossy and pretty as you see it in the store. This finish is had by varnishing. But before this it has a "button" woven on it if it should demand that style of finish.

Here the young ladies come to the front, and by their deftness of finger weave on what is called a button, but which we should say was linen thread glued into strips that look like nothing so much as shavings of whalebone. These buttons are what you admire as ornaments near the butt of the whip, and further up the stock so placed as to define the handle.

At this point the order for that hundred dozen has become scattered all over the works, because the finish and ornaments called for are various.

While the buttoning is going on some others require metal "caps" and "ferules."

Off in one corner is a little factory that is doing business on its own account. Here the metal, precious and common, is spun up, impressed by steel dies carrying a multiplicity of patterns, and made into ferules and caps.

There are thousands of dollars' worth of property in expensive dies. and the precious metals here worked up, and

ALL IN THE SOLE INTEREST OF ORNAMENTS.

Sometimes it is expensive to please the eye in whips as in other things.

These ornaments are applied and again this simple whip is
eated tc waterproofing and varnishing, and hung up by its neck
•r a long dry.

I forgot to say that damp is the kind of grippe that is fatal to
hips And somewhat ahead of the processes last described, it is
eated for damp by practitioners of experience.

No fond mother could rear up its child any more carefully than
this whip encased in buckskin, or rawhide or metal foil to keep
ιe damp away from the interior. No lead filling waterproofing,
arnishing, is omitted that will stand between "its little in sides"
ιd the cold, cold world.

It is truly wonderful, when you think of it, what you buy in a
ollar whip!

Finally it is ready for the snap. A snap is a simple thing - to
ιok at It would astonish you to know the it formerly gave the whip
ιaker. After he learned the trick of weaving it, it had to be learned
ι put it on so that it would stay put. Tie it, you say. Certainly, and
ιat is what they did. But it had an unpleasant habit of coming
ntied and dropping off. Here again the ingenious mind got in its
ne work. An old employe studied the problem, and by a simple
ttle turn and twist of the snap or lash made a peculiar knot that
·ill wear out a whip in durability.

An interesting circumstance about this great factory is called to
ιind by the snap incident. It is the fact that whole families have, in
ϸme instances, to the second and third generation, been employed
ι this one factory, and thus

ONG AND INTELLIGENT FAMILIARITY

with whip making has led to the overcoming of obstacles, the
ιvention of devices and machinery that could hardly otherwise
.ave seen the light. Who can say how far we would have been from
ιe twenty-five-cent whip, but for this intelligent Yankee thought
ιat is never content unless "improving" something?

The whips on my order are now beginning to come into the
eservation down stairs in dozens, and are being accounted for
y their tags and a perfect record that appears in a book in the
ιipping room. They have been labeled with fancy names, mean-
ιme; some even have the name of the dealer to whom they are

going woven in by the deft fingers of those young ladies wh
are so expert at "buttoning," and now, by quarter dozens, the
are wrapped in manilla papers, assembled, marked, boxed an
shipped.

I return to the office with the tag I started out with, the tag nov
looking like Jacob's coat of many colors, and I rest myself by askin
a few simple questions. I want to know, for instance,

HOW MANY DIFFERENT STYLES OF WHIPS

the American Whip Company make. I am told upward of on
thousand. I also want to know the greatest number of whips fir
ished in one day; that is, bow many come out of the factory, read
to ship. The answer is 1,226 dozen, that 4,200 dozen come out in
week, and 15,000 dozen in a month.

I thought I bad
enough of statistics, the
figures were getting too
bewildering; but I feel
sure all who read of what
I saw, when next they
see, buy, handle or sell a
whip, will have a higher
regard for the genius that
could make its existence
possible.

American Whip Company—Officers.

C.H.E.R.

In closing the pages devoted to this most remarkable corpora
tion, it may be of interest to many to know the names of men nc
already mentioned, who assist in directing its affairs. The New Yor
store is under the management of W.J. Cassard, also a director c
the company, with N.J. Davis, T.J. Horan and J.H.B. Dawson o
the road, assisted in the office by George Wright as bookkeepe
The Chicago store is presided over by W.C. Pease, also director (

eteran salesman), with L.W. Jones whose headquarters are at St. Paul, Mich.; Chas. F. Clark of Belvidere, Ill.; W. F. Baker, Greenville, Ohio; J. A. St. Clair, Kansas City, Mo.; W.E. Hall, Evanston, Ill.; F.S. Clements, Jackson, Mich., with C.W. Cleveland in charge of the office.

The San Francisco house is managed ably by the Keystone Brothers, who were formerly in the employ of the company in their boyhood, at Westfield.

The traveling salesmen are Curtis Nelson (over forty years a traveler and stockholder of the company); D. F. Dunham, Boston, Mass., F. A. Nelson, Buffalo, N. Y., D. R. Putnam of Brandon, Vt.

For the past five years the officers and directors of the company have been: L.R. Norton, Hon. E.B. Gillett, D.L. Gillett, Horace W. Avery, S.F. Shepard, D.C. Hull, L.M. Osden, R.T. Sherman, Lewis Parker, Ira Miller, all of Westfield, Mass.; W. Pease, Chicago, Ills.; C.W. Darling and W.J. Cassard of New York.

Appendix B

Westfield, "the Whip City"

WESTERN NEW ENGLAND

VOL. 1   FEBRUARY, 1911   NO. 3

The Whip City of the World

A Sketch of the Industry which was Originated and Developed in Westfield, where about Eighty-five Per Cent of All the Whips are Made—A Hint of the Saving in Time that Three Million Whips a Year can Make

By Edwin W. Newdick

The rapid development of this country must be due in some appreciable measure to Westfield. The United States is the wonder of the world because of the rapidity of its growth. Westfield, maybe, deserves a good part of the credit for this. Now Westfield, in spite of its numerous busy industries, is a peaceful town; but in the midst of this peaceful, beautiful community has been produced during the past century what must have been, collectively considered, a great factor in the country's speed of accomplishment; for in Westfield have been made during the past century enough millions of whips to make a saving of centuries of time as a result of their application. Whips are made over there now at the rate of close to a million and a half dozens annually. People haven't all taken to automobiles evidently. As a matter of fact there were more than twenty horse-drawn vehicles manufactured in this country last year for every single automobile made, according to figures published by an auto-

THE BUSINESS STREET IN THE TOWN WHERE MOST OF THE WORLD'S WHIPS ARE MADE

THE PLANT OF THE BIGGEST WHIP MANUFACTURERS IN THE WORLD, THE UNITED STATES WHIP COMPANY

(The head offices and all the manufacturing plants are at Westfield, except the building shown at the extreme left of the picture, which is the company's branch at Sidney, Ohio)

IN THE RATTAN STORAGE HOUSE OF THE UNITED STATES WHIP COMPANY, THE WORLD'S LARGEST WHIP PRODUCERS

ANOTHER VIEW IN THE WESTFIELD FACTORY OF THE UNITED STATES WHIP COMPANY

mobile magazine. It is estimated that eighty thousand automobiles were made in this country in 1910 while the estimate for horse-drawn vehicles is almost a million and three-quarters.

Nearly all of the development from those crude affairs to the whip of today—made by a hundred processes and of materials from the ends of the earth and the depths of the sea—has been made in Westfield. And all in order that more haste may be made! Just imagine—if each whip made results in the saving of ten minutes during its service as haste inducer, then the product of all the factories of Westfield for a year would mean a saving of more than four hundred years of time; and if in ten minutes a ton can be moved a half mile, then, in a single year, Westfield's contribution to the world's time-saving devices results in the saving of enough time in which to move the whole earth (which weighs but four thousand six hundred forty-three trillions of tons) about one seven-thousandth of an inch!

Whips have been in demand for centuries and crude affairs that served for "beating" and "smiting" were used 'way back in Bible times and in Kings "whip" is mentioned. But the things used were not more than the rod which Saint Paul admonished against sparing. We know of the horrible cruelties inflicted by the lashed whips used up to a century ago for administering punishment or inflicting persecution. But a real snapping, curling, stinging "licking" was never possible with the maximum of sting and the maximum of wound until Westfield produced whips. And for years Westfield has made whips in countless thousands and of a thousand different sizes and styles. Westfield has, to a degree that is equalled in few cases, the distinction not only of leading an industry, but of having made it. Westfield has bred practically all the men who have been and are important in the in-

dustry; in Westfield—and by Westfield men—have been invented, developed and improved the intricate and ingenious machines by which whips are made.

When one tickles Dobbin on the flank with the whip that stands in the carriage socket, one doesn't think any more about it, if Dobbin responds. Man has much more impatience than thirst for knowledge and, if Dobbin

THE UNITED STATES WHIP FACTORY MAKES DAILY AN AVERAGE OF ABOUT TWENTY-FIVE THOUSAND WHIPS

THE PLAITING ROOM IN THE UNITED STATES WHIP COMPANY'S FACTORY

A FEW OF THE FINISHED WHIPS IN THE STOCK ROOM OF THE UNITED STATES WHIP COMPANY

hastens, what matter is it that contributions to that saving of time were made from Arctic to Equator and from here to the Orient?

There are something like a hundred operations to making a whip. If one is interested in manufacturing processes, it is fascinating to study the making of whips. The common species of whips, the straight kind commonly used in carriages, are made in dozens of varieties of materials. The basic materials are usually rattan and rawhide. Whalebone used to be used for the "centers" of whips but it is now too expensive. It used to cost, in the early days, from twenty-five to thirty-five cents a pound but now one must pay from nine dollars to ten dollars a pound for it.

York. These religious people were the first to cut strands from horsehide by stripping. The simple whips, made of a hickory rod and a lash hitched to the rod by a loop, were considerably improved after a while. After Jokes had been making these lashed whips a short time, others began making them. Boiling the whips in different oils was tried and considered as making a great improvement. Those boiled were called "twisted whips." These were made of white oak and other woods and often covered with black sheepskin sewed on over the wooden stock.

The Father of the Whip Industry

Hiram Hull is sometimes called "the father of the whip industry." A whip maker, Aaron Phelps, encountered

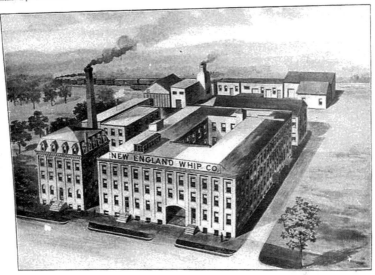

THE FACTORY OF THE NEW ENGLAND WHIP COMPANY

The Jokes that Started Whip Making

Jokes started the whip industry in Westfield. Joseph was his first name. Joseph Jokes lived, moved and had his being in Westfield. He had a choice lot of hickory, we are told, and had also, we are led to conclude, a fair amount of Yankee thrift. He discovered that his choice lot of hickory was making him some quasi-friends who called around to get (free) some of the hickory from Mr. Jokes' lot; but the hickory wasn't making him any money. The friends of Mr. Jokes found that the hickory with which he obliged them made excellent whip stocks. Jokes tried making some whip stocks himself and offering them for sale. Then he put a horsehide lash on each, securing the lash to the stock by a "keeper." These were the first whips made in Westfield.

Strands for lashes were first cut on flat tables; then came a contribution from the Shakers of Lebanon, New

Hull in Windsor, Conn., and thought he would be a valuable man for Westfield's leading industry, so prevailed upon him to go there. Hiram Hull made many inventions and improvements which meant much to the whip industry and without which the development of the industry would have been greatly delayed. David C. Hull, a son of Hiram, still works for the United States Whip Company, although now eighty-two years old. He is one of the oldest whip makers in the country and perhaps the oldest still in the business. Mr. David Hull has himself made important inventions and improvements which are used by the United States and other whip companies. Hull & Son, Hiram and David, were the predecessors of the Harrison Whip Company from which the American Whip Company developed and the latter is, more than any other, the parent company of the United States Whip Company, the largest in the world.

The first plaited whip (a whip with a cover of cotton, silk or other fibre woven on over the whip) is said to have been made by one D. L. Farnham in the cabinet shop of Erastus Grant. Pieces of rattan were glued around whalebone and the whole covered—the exact principles of present-day whip making, although whalebone is largely superseded by rawhide and other materials.

The Process of Plaiting

Plaiting is a difficult process to do by hand. It is easy to imagine the difficulty of tieing a number of threads to the end of a whip and then weaving these threads over the entire length of the whip. The first plaiting "machine" was composed of a barrel, a number of small weights and one large one. The large weight was tied to a cord which passed over a pulley and was then attached to the small

each other at full speed with never an accident. Imagine a circle of figure 8's placed end to end with cars tearing around in both directions, over switches and past each other with never a halt or a hesitation—then you get an idea of a plaiting machine in action. The bobbins, each carrying a thread attached to the whip which they all travel around, run 'round and 'round, in and out and past each other weaving the threads for the covering of the whip. These plaiting machines were introduced from Germany and England. A machine was found in Providence which braided shoestrings and Hiram Hull, who saw it, realized its possibilities for the whip industry. The patent rights were bought for a thousand dollars. The machines, though not a New England invention, were developed in New England and in Westfield, to a new usefulness and nicety of operation.

THE FINE PLANT OF THE INDEPENDENT WHIP COMPANY

end of the whip, holding it upright and drawing it up as the workmen wove the threads over the whip. All these threads, as many as a dozen or, often, a score, were attached to the tip of the whip and hung down around the outside of the barrel inside of and above which the whip was suspended. At the end of each thread was one of the small weights. The plaiting was done by moving the threads about, each being held in the place desired by the weight at the end of it.

Now the plaiting is done by a wonderfully simple and ingenious machine that reminds one of nothing more than a single-track railway system with numerous turnouts operating a series of cars on a race track. And oh, for a railway system which would keep so accurately to schedule! For the cars on this system (which are bobbins) race around and around (they all run express) and pass

Material from Jungle and Ocean

But to begin with the rattan—this comes from India; it used to be brought over in ships as packing, to fill in the crevices so the cargo wouldn't rattle and move about; where the ships were unloaded the rattan was thrown out on the wharves to be had for the picking up. But now rattan costs a tidy little sum and the United States Whip Company, the largest of the many companies in Westfield, alone uses about six hundred tons of rattan a year. The rawhide comes "green" from South America and India, some of it being from the India Buffalo. It is tanned, cut and twisted before it is ready for the whip-making processes. The new hide is twisted and allowed to dry. It is then unevenly round and nearly as big as a pencil. Then it is put through machines that smooth it off and make it evenly round. The chips and dust from the rawhide are used for making glue.

The hide of a fish is being used to some extent instead of horsehide. One popular brand of whips, the "Sirenia," is named from a species to which the fish belongs. The "sea-cow" is the commonest name for the animal, this name being applied because the sea-cow feeds on weeds and is a mammal, producing milk for its young. It is claimed that the mermaid was a name applied to this animal or a superstitious belief roused by this animal. The sea-cow is also called dugong and manatee.

The Making of Whips

Meanwhile the rattan has been having an exciting time of it. After being sorted and dried, the thin outer

workman wiggles the whip in nonchalant ease, lays it on the bench beside him, rubs a plane here and there once or twice and the whip is as evenly balanced as one wishes.

Here is where an important variation in manufacture is made, depending on the quality of the particular whip being made. The rattan of the best whips is covered with sheet rubber which is then vulcanized. This gives a waterproof covering that adds to the resiliency of the whip and adds several fold to the life of the whip besides. The whips are then ready for the plaiting room where the cover is woven on them, a piece of iron or steel having been previously put in the stock for weight, called the "load." After the plaiting, the coats of filling are put on, then the whips get several baths in varnish, then, when the buttons, ferrules and mountings are on and the snap-

ANOTHER OF WESTFIELD'S BIG WHIP FACTORIES, THE H. M. VAN DEUSEN WHIP COMPANY

covering is taken off. Then the rattan is cut up into pieces that will fit around the rawhide center of the whips. The rattan goes into one end of a machine and squirts out the other end at a great speed, cut to the required sizes. Eight of these pieces of rattan are put around a hide or whalebone center, dipped in nice, warm, oozy glue, then bound together in a twinkling with a piece of rope around them to hold them tightly until the glue dries. Westfield's largest company uses about a hundred tons of glue each year.

Another machine takes the glued-together rattan strips and, with a buzz and a zip not so long as a lover's sigh, turns the rattan out rounded and tapering and beginning to look as if it would soon be a whip. Then comes a chance for the most experienced workmen. This is "taking out the jumps." A whip may be straight and even-appearing but when held by the butt and tried, it does not bend evenly—it has a "jump" in it. The expert

pers attached, the whip is ready for the shipping-room.

It is astonishing to know the quantities of material that go into the whips made in a single year. An idea can be gained from the amount used by a single concern, the United States Whip Company. In a single year this company uses, in round numbers, approximately seventy-five tons of thread, three hundred thousand yards of cotton cloth, one hundred tons of iron (for the "load" in the butt), one hundred and eighty-five thousand pounds of hides, five hundred thousand feet of lumber for packing cases, eighteen thousand gallons of varnish and seventy-five carloads of wood used for the butts of the cheap whips.

Whip Companies of Fifty Years Ago

In 1855 there were about thirty whip companies in Westfield. Some facts about each of the eight leaders at that time are given below:—

Name	Age	Number of Hands	Yearly Value of Output
Dow & Gillett	15 years	100	$55,000
J. & R. Noble	20 "	100	50,000
William Robins & Co.	20 "	100	25,000
H. Harrison & Co.	28 "	350	150,000
J. R. Rand Co.	20 "	70	50,000
King & Avery	2 "	10	8,000
R. Loomis & Co.	2 "	15	20,000
Munroe, Brownson & Co.	5 "	30	30,000

The largest of these concerns, H. Harrison & Company, was succeeded by the American Whip Company which was to a considerable degree the nucleus about which, in 1892, fourteen companies were merged into the United States Whip Company. The company is capitalized at a million dollars, four hundred thousand dollars in preferred and the rest in common stock. The company

Large and Growing Westfield Companies

The plant occupied by the New England Whip Company has been enlarged during the past year and its equipment improved so that it now has an ample amount of modern machinery to meet the demands of a prosperous and fast-increasing business. The company now does a volume of business annually that totals about three-quarters of a million dollars, close to a quarter of the whip business done in Westfield where approximately eighty-five per cent. of the whips made in the country are manufactured. The New England company uses electricity exclusively for light and power throughout its plant. The company has a number of ingenious machines which have been developed in its factory, some of which are used there exclusively. The company has been organized about twenty years. Its remarkable growth has brought it to the position of being the largest concern in the country, which is the development from a single company. The company's goods and policy have enabled them to secure good customers

THE NEW FACTORY OF THE HORSE WHIP COMPANY

makes close to half the whips used in the country and its factory at Westfield is the largest whip factory in the world. The company owns another big factory at Sidney, Ohio. Westfield must make more than seventy-five per cent of all the whips made in this country and probably nearer ninety per cent.

Mr. George E. Whipple, the president of this large company, is active in its management and one of the best known of Westfield's many men who are prominent whip makers. Mr. Whipple has been connected with the whip business in one capacity and another since his boyhood. For years he managed the George E. Whipple Company which made mountings and ferrules for most of the whip factories. Mr. Whipple was president of the Peck & Whipple Company which was absorbed by the United States Whip Company. He has been prominent in the affairs of the United States Company ever since its formation and for the past twelve years has been at its head.

in almost every city of importance in this country. The company has a present capacity of about twenty thousand whips per day. Its officers are experienced, efficient and progressive. Eugene Doherty is president and Daniel F. Doherty, secretary, treasurer and general manager of the company.

The Independent Whip Company is one of the most prosperous in Westfield and this, in the whip industry, means in the country. Its factory might well serve as a model for a whip factory. It was completed seven years ago, is excellently equipped and makes possible a surprisingly large output, because of the remarkable efficiency and economy with which it can be operated. The company was organized in 1894 and incorporated a year later. The company manufactures a general line of whips and has built up an invaluable reputation for the quality and good value of its product. Agents of the company cover the United States and in addition the concern does quite an export trade, particularly in Canada, Mexico, South

America, Cuba, Germany and other countries. J. H. Bryan is president, F. E. Cowles is vice-president and general manager and W. H. Russell is treasurer. The concern is rapidly forging ahead and its place as one of Westfield's best is now assured.

Cargill, Cleveland and Company is one of the old concerns of Westfield. Its company has a complete factory, doing all the manufacturing processes, making a full line of whips, but making a specialty of high grade English crops, sticks, coach-whips and so forth. Wilber G. Cargill, one of the best known whip men on the road, is the senior member of the company and he himself personally visits the large jobbing trade to which practically all of the company's product goes. Harvey Cleveland, the junior member of the company, is at the head of the manufacturing.

The Horse Whip Company has recently built a new factory in Westfield which was occupied two years ago. The company has been organized about nine years but it became necessary to enlarge the manufacturing space, so a new building was erected and occupied with the addition of a lot of new machinery. The company makes a specialty of its "Zebu Azo" whip which has a large sale. M. M. Broga is president of the company. He was a traveling man for many years succeeding 1870. C. J.

Bradley is general manager of the concern and Charles W. Vayo is vice-president.

The Standard Whip Company is one of the old companies of Westfield, although there have been many changes in the concern since 1892. The business was actually started about 1865. The last two years have seen a doubling of the company's business and this concern is bound to be of increasing importance in the industry. J. C. McCarthy is president and general manager and Charles J. Rooney is treasurer and sales manager. The company has been in its new quarters only about three months but already its increased capacity and improved facilities have had their effects in enlarging the business.

Another of the large independent concerns is Steiner & Moore Whip Company, incorporated in 1889. Now it is one of the busy whip-making plants in the town and has a business and a reputation that extends all over the United States. This company makes all kinds of whips, including the rawhide, the wire center and the rubber-lined whip. They also make a great many Java whips, and do a large business on what they term the "Vibrator" whip which has a tempered steel wire run through the entire length, to give the whip strength and elasticity.

Westfield has altogether nearly two score of companies making whips, accessories for whip making and whip-making machinery.

A Plea for a Clean River

A Possible Solution of the Problem Suggested—Relation of the Subject to Conservation Shown

By Albert W. Cobb

Abraham Lincoln said, early in his public career: "To make two blades of grass grow where one grew before; to pluck from life a thistle and in its place to plant a flower—this shall be my aim." Far more easily now amid good-will and coöperative good-fellowship, can this principle, so simply stated by Abraham Lincoln, be applied by our people of Massachusetts along their superb valley of the Connecticut river from the north bound to the south bound of our Commonwealth.

The one surpassing lesson this generation needs to heed and act on quickly is that of peace; to eliminate from the methods of nations the element of armed warfare and instead apply money and labor to developing and fructifying the earth; to increasing and multiplying the people and making them healthier and happier. The hideous fallacy of Malthus, which has obtained too

long, can be disproved by devoting to the healthful distributing and maintenance of human life the resources which have been and are still being applied to restricting and destroying human welfare and life by war. The cost of one battleship would easily provide for right utilization of the Connecticut river valley from the headwaters to Long Island Sound with all the essential equipment for sewerage reform and fertilized farming, navigation and fisheries, making the valley of "the Rhine of America" more bountifully fruitful, more thoroughly healthful and more gloriously beautiful. An important step toward the beginning of such a fine and progressive benefit to the section and example to the country has been made by the bill providing for an investigation and report by experts. The bill, introduced by Senator John F. Malley of Hampden, is as follows:—

SPRINGFIELD FROM ACROSS THE RIVER

Appendix C
Cargill, Cleveland & Company Catalog

Illustrated Catalog

Cargill, Cleveland & Company

Makers of FINE WHIPS

Westfield, Mass., U. S. A.

TERMS.

90 days net or 5 per cent. 10 days from date of invoice.

All goods F. O. B. our depot, no charge being made for boxing or drayage.

Our prices are by the dozen.

Be particular and give the length and number wanted.

Cargill, Cleveland & Co.

STRAIGHT JAVA WHIPS.

No. 50.
Java stock, black polished handle, loop snap, made in 5, 5½ and 6 ft.

No. 63.
Java stock, nail cap, plaited black, made in 4 1-3, 5, 5½ and 6 ft.

No. 85s.
Java stock, 2 Philadelphia buttons, Boston snap, made in three colors, 5½ and 6 ft.

No. 160.
One piece of rattan, plaited black, with our patent finish, made in 6 feet only; 2 Phila. buttons.

No. 151.
All reed whip, patent black finish, Jap cap, heavy load, 2 Phila. buttons, 5½ and 6 ft., Boston snap.

No. 153.
All reed whip, patent black finish, Jap cap, heavy load, 5½, 6 ft., Phila. buttons, socket guard, Boston snap.

No. 165.
All reed whip, heavily loaded, patent black, 2-one inch buttons, Boston snap, 5½ and 6 ft.

3

No. 155.

All reed whip, heavily loaded, patent finish, 1 inch head button, 1 inch thumb button and 2 Phila. buttons, Boston snap, made in 5½ and 6 ft.

No. 170.

All black, loaded whip, Phila, snap, a big seller, 5½ and 6 ft.

No. 162.

OUR LEADER, "EARLY BIRD" whip, black patent finished, patent load, rubber cushion cap, made in 4 1-3, 5, 5½, 6, 6½ and 7 ft.

No. 203.

"OUR QUEEN", black heavy load, rubber cap, 1 inch buttons, made in 4 1-3, 5, 5½, 6, 6½ and 7 ft.

No. 157.

Heavy loaded, one piece reed whip, made in three colors, black, wine and fair, imitation leather handle, 2 hand made buttons, rubber cap, made in 6 ft. only.

No. 195.

Black full stocked, patent finish, buck and metallic lined, 2 Phila buttons, rubber cushion cap, Phila. snap, 5½, 6 and 6½ ft.

Not illustrated.

No. 204. ·

Black, patent finish, full stocked, buck and metallic lined, 18 inch wound celluloid center, Phila. snap, 6 ft. only.

4

OUR HIGH GRADE STRAIGHT RAWHIDE WHIPS.

No. 114.

This whip contains one solid piece of rawhide from snap through handle, patent finish, 6 ft. only.

No. 101.

Heavily loaded, rawhide through handle, black patent finish. 2 two-inch buttons. 5½ and 6 ft.

No. 109.

Half length rawhide, patent black finish, rubber cap, made in 7 ft. only.

No. 120N.

"OUR COMMON SENSE". ½ length rawhide, solid rubber cap, full stocked, patent finish, made in all lengths.

No. 0120½.

Full stocked, ½ length rawhide, leather handle, 2 hand made buttons, strictly waterproof, made in 6, 6½ and 7 ft.

No. 142.

Black, full stocked, full length rawhide from snap through handle, no splicing, heavily loaded handle, made in 6 ft. only.

No. 138.

"SILVER DOLLAR" rawhide, wire under cover, good size, rawhide running from snap through handle, heavy load, patent finish, made in 5½, 6, 6½ and 7 ft.

5

OUR HIGH GRADE STRAIGHT RAWHIDE WHIPS—Con.

No. 131.

"OUR RUSSIAN" rawhide, black, best quality, 7-12 length rawhide, double cover, 2½ inch black chased ferrules, rubber cushion cap, made in 5, 5½, 6, 6½ and 7 ft.

No. 129.

OUR RUBBER LINED RAWHIDE, black, best quality of stock, 7-12 best center, rubber lined from snap to handle, gut loop, made in 4 1-3, 5, 5½, 6, 6½ and 7 ft.

No. 124.

"ROYAL ENGLISH" Rawhide, black, best quality, 7-12 center, double cover, double loop, 2 one-inch and 5 Phila. buttons, rubber cushion cap, made in 6½ ft. only.

No. 0121.

Black, ½ length rawhide, 1½ inch nickel head and 1½ inch ferrules and 9 ¾ inch plain nickel ferrules, made in 6½ and 7 ft.

No. 145.

Black finish, nickel spring wire, wound center, two thread covers, gut loop, 7-12 best center, 2 2¼ inch buttons, made in all lengths.

No. X136.

"OUR HIGH TEST" Rawhide, best rawhide to handle, two thread covers, 2 fine hand made buttons, rubber cushion cap, gut loop, made in 4 1-3 to 8 ft.

No. 130.

"OK" Rawhide, rawhide to handle, rubber lined center, full length of whip, two thread covers, gut loop, BEST WHIP MADE, 5 to 7 ft.

6

OUR CELEBRATED WHALEBONE WHIPS.

No. 304.

Black, full stocked, ½ length solid piece of whalebone, linen lined, Jap cap, 2 Phila. buttons, made in 5½, 6, 6½ and 7 ft.

No. 303.

Black, full stocked, ½ length whalebone, rubber cap, Phila. buttons, buck lined, made in 5½, 6, 6½ and 7 ft.

No. 339.

Gent's road wagon whip, best ½ bone, turned small, buck lined, 2 fine hand made buttons, made in 5, 5½, 6, 6½ and 7 ft.

No. 340.

Black, best quality ½ whalebone, two thread covers, fine finish, Phila. buttons, rubber cap, made in all lengths from 4 1-3 to 8 ft.

No. 368.

Best 2-3 whalebone, buck lined, hand made buttons, fine quality, made in all lengths from 5 to 8 ft.

No. 380.

Best bone to handle, buck lined, fine hand made buttons, "Good Feelers", made in all lengths.

No. 390.

Black, bone to handle, Phila. buttons, rubber cap, GREAT WHIP FOR THE MONEY, made in 6, 6½ and 7 ft.

7

No. 333.

Imitation gut plait, extra heavy ½ bone, double cover, 9 inch leather handle, 2 eight stitch buttons, rubber cushion, made in 6 ft. only.

No. 343.

Best ½ bone, imitation gut cover, 9 inch pig handle. 2 needle stitch buttons. rubber cushion cap, English snap, made in 6 ft. only.

No. 310.

Black, half bone, buck lined, 1½ inch nickel head and 1½ inch nickel ferrule, and 9 ¾ inch ferrules, made in 7 ft. only.

No. 400.

Fine quality brown malacca, bone top, linen color, plain German silver head and ferrule, made in 6, 6½ and 7 ft.

No. 631.

German malacca, linen color. bone top. fine pig handle. plain head and ferrule. made in 6 ft. only.

No. 308.

Black, ½ whalebone, buck lined, 10 inch alligator handle. hand made head button, and 1½ inch hand chased ferrule, rubber cushion cap, made only in 6 ft.

No. 307.

Same as No. 308, except that it has a lizard skin handle.

8

OUR CELEBRATED WHALEBONE WHIPS—Con.

No. 330.

"GENUINE GUT COVER", best ½ whalebone, double cover, six stitch buttons, rubber cap, English snap, made in 6, 6½ and 7 ft.

No. 327.

Best ½ whalebone, ebony handle, chased gold ferrule, 6, 6½ and 7 ft.

No. 329.

Same as No. 327, except that it has a snake wood handle.

No. 358.

Best ½ bone, fancy English celluloid handle, silver ferrules, made in 6 ft. only.

No. 357.

Same as No. 358, except that it has an imitation gut cover.

No. 378.

Best full bone to handle, gut cover, hand made buttons, made in all lengths.

No. 379.

Same as No. 378, except that it has a Russian leather handle.

9

OUR CELEBRATED WHALEBONE WHIPS—Con.

No. 460.

Extra large BARE BONE, black smooth rubber finish, three six stitch sash buttons, rubber cap, made in 6, 6½ and 7 ft.

No. 466.

Extra large BARE BONE, black finish, ebony handle with 1½ inch tapered plain roll gold ferrule, made in 6. 6½ and 7 ft.

No. 462.

Extra large BARE BONE, 10 inch carved celluloid handle, two 1½ inch roll gold ferrules hand chased, made in 6½ ft. only.

No. 461.

Extra large BARE BONE, knotted in clusters, ivory setting in 68 knots, celluloid handle, 1½ inch roll gold ferrule, made in 6 and 6½ ft.

No. 468.

Extra large BARE BONE, knotted in clusters, ivory setting in knots, 10 inch ivory handle, fine roll gold ferrule, 6½ ft. only.

We manufacture 40 other styles of fancy BARE BONE whips.

TRACK WHIPS.

4 1-3 ft. long ; regulation length.

No. 0193.

Black, all rattan whip, two 1 inch buttons, rubber cap.

No. 442.

Black, stocked ½ length rawhide, Phila. buttons, rubber cap.

No. 443.

Linen color, rawhide center, 8 inch leather handle, Phila. buttons, rubber cap.

10

Appendix C   105

No. 450.

Black, best one-half bone, double cover, rubber cap.

No. 452.

Black, best two-thirds bone, double cover.

No. 454.

Black, best full bone whip, double cover.

No. 453.

Full bone hog handle, English snap, imitation gut cover.

We have 18 other styles of track whips.

STAGE STALKS.

No. 510.

Plain white hickory, buck keepers, made in 2½, 3, 3½, 4, 4½ and 5 ft.

No. 500.

Same as No. 510, with the exception that it is hand shaved.

Not illustrated.

No. 523.

Black, rawhide center, 1½ inch nickel head and nine ¾-inch nickel ferrules, made in 3½, 4, 4½ ft.

Not illustrated.

No. 520.

Black, one-half bone, 1½ inch nickel head and ferrule, four, ¾ inch nickel ferrules, buck keepers, made in 4 and 4½ ft.

No. 524.

Best FULL BONE, 2½ inch nickel head and 3 ferrules, made in 4, 4½ and 5 ft.

Not illustrated.

We have several other styles not described here.

11

CAB, EXPRESS AND TEAM WHIPS.

All drop tops.

No. 245¾.
Mixed color the entire length, smooth finish, no trimmings, nail cap, 2¾ ft. stalk, 5¼ ft. entire length.

No. 275.
Mixed linen color, Jap cap, 1 inch head and thumb button, 3½ ft. stalk, 3 ft. drop.

No. 244.
Mixed linen color, painted black handle, tack end, 1½ inch nickel ferrule, 3 ft. stalk, 3 ft. drop.

No. 252.
Imitation linen mixed color, painted black or red handle, 1 inch nickel head and 1½ inch nickel ferrule, loop snap, 3½ ft. stalk, 3 ft. drop.

No. 241.
Wire plaited cover, two 1-inch buttons, solid rubber cap, loop snap, 3½ ft. stalk, 3 ft. drop.

No. 231.
Black plaited JUMBO, tack end, large heavy stalk, 2 ft. drop, 4½ and 5 ft.

No. 231¾.
Same as No. 231, with the exception that it is linen color.

Not illustrated.

No. 250.
Black, 4 plait cab, round leather lash, plaited in top, extending 13 inches, plain 1½ inch nickel head and ferrule, 3½ ft. stalk, 3 ft. drop.

12

CAB, EXPRESS AND TEAM WHIPS—Con.

No. 224.

Extra heavy milk wagon whip, plaited imitation linen, 5 ft. stalk, 5 ft. drop, 1½ inch black metal head and 2¾ inch black ferrule, 10 ft. entire length.

No. 222.

Mixed color, spiral plait, 12 inch painted black handle, 1 inch nickel head, 4½ ft. stalk, 2½ ft. drop.

No. 91.

Wine color stalk, 3 ft. lash, plait drop, 5 ft. stalk, plain 1 inch nickel head and 1½ inch ferrule.

No. 262.

Wine color, 5 ft. stalk, 3 ft. lash, plait drop, three 1 inch buttons, 5 Phila. buttons, also made with 5½ ft. stalk and 4 ft. drop.

No. 260.

Black, plaited cover with 4 plait horse hide lash top, stalk 2½, 3, 3½, 4 ft.; 1 inch nickel head, 1½ inch nickel ferrule.

No. 269.

Black plaited rawhide express, two 1 inch black buttons, Jap cap, made in 3½ and 4 ft.

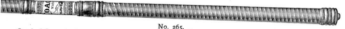

No. 265.

Stocked Java, fancy plait, 1 inch chased head, 1½ inch nickel ferrule, 5½ ft. stalk, 5 ft. imitation lash top, 6 nickel buttons.

13

ENGLISH HOLLYS, MALACCAS AND OAKS—Con.

No. 1462.
Genuine English holly, imitation pig handle, tapered head and ferrule, 6 plait English top.

No. 1465.
Genuine English holly, imitation thorn stick, leather handle, nickel head and ferrule, 6 plait top.

No. 1469.
Genuine English holly, pig skin handle, well knotted stalk, 6 plait top.

No. 1479.
Genuine English holly, extra knotted, pig handle, silver head and ferrule, 6 plait top.

No. 1477.
Genuine English holly, well knotted, hog skin handle, plaited extension bone top, linen color, 1½ inch silver head and ferrule.

No. 1476.
Genuine English holly, extra knotted, fancy alligator handle, plain silver head and ferrule, fine English quilled top.

Not illustrated.

No. 1487.
Genuine English holly, dark or light color, extra large knots, fine calf skin handle, silver head and ferrule, fine 6 plait top.

18

No. 257.

Stocked rawhide, black plaited cover, Jap cap, two 1 inch buttons, horsehide top, made in 3½, 4½, and 5 ft.

No. 257½.

Same as No. 257 with the exception that it has 1 inch nickel head and 5 short nickel ferrules.

No. 256.

Russet, 6 plait hand braided lace leather cover, 10 inch leather handle, buck stitch, rawhide through handle, 2 russet hand buttons, made in 4½ ft. only.

No. 183.

Leather covered rawhide stalk, horsehide lash, Jap cap, two 1 inch buttons, made in 4½ ft. only.

No. 258.

Heavy full stocked rawhide, plaited black, 5 nickel buttons, 1 inch nickel head, 6 plait buck lash, made in 5 ft.

No. 239.

Black heavy one-half whalebone, 12 inch leather handle, 6 plait buck top, 2½ inch chased nickel head, two 2½ inch nickel ferrules, made in 4½, 5, 5½ ft.

No. 187.

XX oil tanned buck stitched, leather loop and braided buck snap, 2 leather buttons, made in all lengths from 2½ to 6 ft.

We have 50 other styles of Cab and Express Whips.

14

SWIVEL HANDLE DROVE WHIPS.

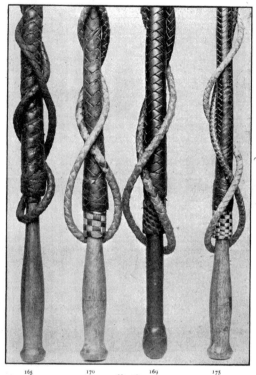

165   170   169   175

No. 165.
Six plait russet braided cover, California style, 10 ft.
No. 170.
Jacksonville, 6 plait braided cover, fancy braided button, made in 10 and 12 ft.
No. 169.
Jacksonville, 6 plait hand braided cover, shot loaded leather covered handle, hand leather buttons, horsehide point, 10 and 12 ft.
No. 175.
Extra fine Jacksonville, shot loaded, 8 plait hand braided cover, made in 10 and 12 ft.

15

ENGLISH HOLLYS, MALACCAS AND OAKS.

No. 025.

Malacca, brown stalk, plain head and ferrule, thread lash.

No. 025½.

Same as No. 025, with the exception that it has a 6 plait English top.
Not illustrated.

No. 423.

Malacca, small light stalk, plain head and ferrule, 6 plait English top, 5 and 5½ ft. stalk.

No. 420.

Malacca, brown, full knotted, 2 six stitch buttons, rubber cushion cap, 6 plait English top, 5 ft.

No. 110.

Malacca, extra fine quality, large size, knotted, 1¾ inch German silver head and ferrule, 5½ ft.

No. 126.

Malacca, knotted to imitate holly, hand made head button, rubber cushion, 6 plait top, 5½ ft.

No. 140.

Malacca, Birch pattern, full knotted, hand made head button, 6 plait top, 5½ ft.

16

ENGLISH HOLLYS, MALACCAS AND OAKS—Con.

No. 13M.

Malacca, light color, knotted, 6 plait top, 2¼ inch German silver head, 5½ ft.

No. 874M.

Malacca, brown, full knotted, head and thumb button, hand made, fine 6 plait top, 5½ ft.

No. 1149.

Oak, knotted to imitate holly, leather handle, 1½ inch tapered head and ferrule, thread top, English keeper.

No. 0316.

Oak, extra knotted, leather handle, 1½ inch tapered head and ferrule, thread top, pony length.

No. 1455.

Genuine English holly, knotted, brass tapered head, natural bark handle, thread top.

No. 1456.

Same as No. 1455, with an English quilled top.
Not illustrated.

No. 1460.

Genuine English holly, knotted, leather handle, 1½ inch head and ferrule, thread top.

No. 1461.

Genuine English holly, knotted, 4 plait English top, leather handle, 2 tapered ferrules.

17

ENGLISH HOLLYS, MALACCAS AND OAKS—Con.

No. CW172.

Genuine English holly, full knotted, fine calf skin handle, good 6 plait top.

No. CW1.

Genuine English holly, large natural knots, extra fine finish, Russia leather handle, silver head and ferrule, fine 8 plait top.

No. 1498.

Genuine English holly, extra fine, large natural knots, BARE BONE top, Russian leather handle, silver head and ferrule, English quilled top.

No. CW116.

Genuine English holly (four-in-hand), knotted, leather handle, silver ferrule, 12 ft., fine lash.

No. 1311.

Split bamboo stalk, celluloid handle, 2½ inch tapered gold ferrule, fine quilled top.

No. 1312.

Split bamboo stalk, calf skin handle, plain silver head and ferrule, fine lash top.

We have over one hundred other styles of Malaccas and Hollys.

19

ENGLISH HUNTING AND RIDING CROPS.

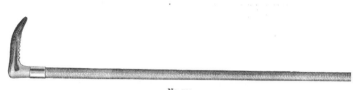

No. 732.

Rawhide center, plaited imitation linen, buck horn head.

No. 733.

Same as No. 732. with the exception that it has short leather handle.

No. 723.

Malacca stalk, buck horn handle, plain silver ferrule.

20

No. 333.

Dark color stalk, sterling silver trimmed, horn head.

No. 722L.

Malacca stalk, 6 inch lizard skin handle, buck horn head, silver ferrule.

No. 128.

Imported stick, bamboo style, buck horn handle, silver ferrule.

21

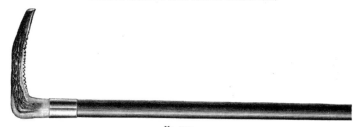

No. 2532.

Malacca, buck horn handle.

No. 3730.

Knotted holly stick, buck horn handle.

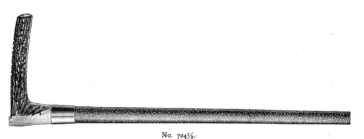

No. 724½.

Rawhide center, pig skin covered stalk, buck horn handle, silver ferrule.

22

No. 2540.

Bone center, genuine gut cover, buck horn handle.

No. 2539.

Bone center, genuine gut cover, short calf leather handle, plain silver ferrule, buck horn head.

No. 731.

Rawhide stalk, pig skin covered, sterling silver trimmed, buck horn handle.
We have 99 other styles, ranging in price from $4.00 to $200.00 per dozen.

23

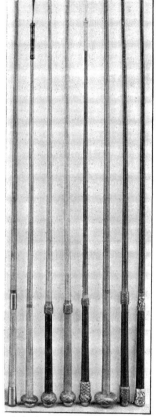

J769 J809½ J210A J216H 734 J765 J755 J766

24

JOCKEY WHIPS.

No. J769.

Rawhide center, linen color, plain gold head and ferrule, English snap.

No. J809½.

Rawhide center, linen color, buck loop, mushroom head button.

No. J210A.

Imitation gut cover, alligator handle, bone center, hand button, apple head, English snap.

No. J210H.

Same as No. J210A, with the exception that it has a hog skin handle.

No. 734.

Imitation gut cover, bone stalk, leather handle, imitation gut buttons, buck loop.

No. J765.

Imitation gut cover, mushroom buttons, English snap, bone center.

No. J755.

Imitation gut cover, Russian leather handle, imitation gut buttons, English snap.

No. J766.

Imitation gut cover, Russian leather handle, bone center, chased silver head and ferrule, English snap.

25

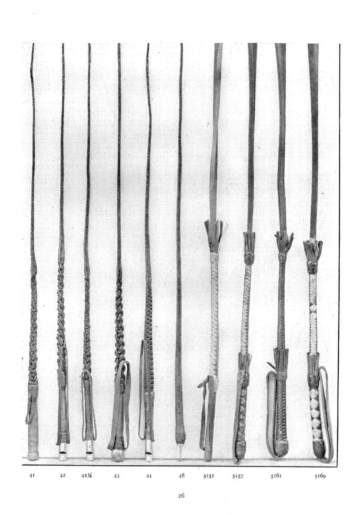

41   42   42½   43   44   48   5151   5157   5161   5169

26

Dog Whips.

No. 40.

Red wire wound handle, russet hand braided cover, 2 buttons.
Not illustrated.

No. 41.

Wood handle, fancy twist braided with loop.

No. 42.

Wood handle with whistle, fancy twist with loop.

No. 42½.

Same as No. 42, with the exception that it has a leather wound handle.

No. 43.

Same as No. 42, with the exception that it has a ball end.

No. 44.

Fancy square braided whistle end with loop.

No. 48.

Fine braided leather with snap end.

Quirts.

No. 5151.

Leather covered iron handle, fancy braid.

No. 5157.

Iron handle, russet and white horsehide diamond plaited handle, 2 frills, 3 buttons.

No. 5161.

Fine 12 plait braided, shot loaded.

No. 5169.

"THE DAISY", shot loaded, 12 plait, white and black calf skin, 2 frills and 3 buttons.

27

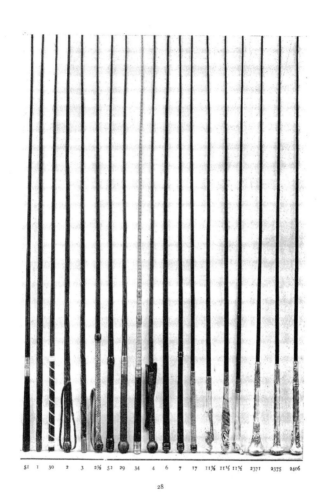

51 1 30 2 3 2½ 52 29 34 4 6 7 17 11⅜ 11⅚ 11⅝ 2371 2375 2406

28

Riding Whips.

No. A.

Fancy plait, 8 inch red handle, wood whistle.

Not illustrated.

No. 31.

Black thread, nickle head and ring.

Not illustrated.

No. 32.

Black thread with horn whistle.

Not illustrated.

No. 51.

Black thread, 6 inch imitation, ebony handle, 1½ inch ferrule.

No. 1.

Painted bare rawhide.

No. 30.

Black thread red handle wound with white cord, 2 white buttons.

No. 2.

Black plaited through rawhide, head button with loop.

No. 3.

Varnished extra rawhide, 1 inch brass head, Boston snap.

No. 2½.

Black plaited handle, solid rawhide, 2 hand buttons with loop.

No. 52.

Black plaited, 6 inch leather handle, 2 hand buttons.

No. 29.

Black, plaited, ball end, nickel ferrule.

No. 34.

Imitation linen color, 6 inch leather handle, nickel head and three chased nickel ferrules.

No. 4.

Painted rawhide, ball end, fancy plait handle with loop.

No. 6.

Black, full stocked rawhide center, Phila. head, with rubber cushion cap, English snap.

No. 7.

Black bone center, Phila. buttons, patent finish.

No. 17.

Black, full whalebone, lizard handle, Phila. head and gold ferrule.

No. 11½.

Black full bone, assorted styles of ivory handles, roll gold ferrule.

Nos. 2371, 2375, 2406.

Black, full whalebone, pearl and sterling silver handle, for very fine trade.

The above is only a small sample of the line of whips which we manufacture. We are pleased to state that we can furnish you with anything that is made in the whip line, as we manufacture somthing like from 800 to 1000 styles. Should you fail to find what you want in this catalogue, if you will kindly write us, describing what you want, we would be only too pleased to take this up with you. We guarantee all our goods just as represented, so if you should want strictly first-class goods at right prices, you should deal with us.

29

Appendix D

Still the Whip City, Harold J Martin, Westfield Whip Mfg. Co., Inc.

Still the Whip City

Westfield takes pride in the diversity of its industry. It was not always so. A century ago whips were its chief industrial product. For many years Westfield made whips, cigars and little else.

The development of a diverse pattern of small industry has been a more recent achievement. Now, with the arrival of the Digital Equipment Corporation, Westfield will cover the manufacturing spectrum from buggy-whips to fourth generation computers. One community's industry could scarcely be more diversified than that.

The newer ventures write their own histories in the glare of present-day publicity, but the engrossing story of Westfield whipmaking has never been fully or authoritatively recorded. What follows is, essentially, only a recital of how Westfield whips are made. Perhaps, if time permits the necessary research, this and succeeding pamphlets may, eventually, constitute the groundwork for a true history of the legendary industry that made Westfield the Whip City of the World.

Harold J. Martin, President

Westfield Whip Mfg. Co., Inc.

For as long as anyone can remember Westfield has been The Whip City. The chances are it always will be. When the whip industry was waning and L. B. Allyn's investigations into food impurities made him a national figure, the town fathers tried calling Westfield "The Pure Food Town." Later, the Chamber of Commerce set out roadside markers calling it "The Friendly City." From time to time inventive souls have coined nicknames involving bicycles, or boilers or sweetness and light. None of them took.

Westfield has been The Whip City ever since 1801 when Titus Pease and Thomas Rose started the whole thing by affixing buckskin thongs to tapered hickory poles and offering them for sale or barter. It is right that it should be. No other name could so succinctly sum up so many fascinating implications. The whip business grew up in an austere New England setting but reached out for exotic materials to the whaling ships, to the India Trade, to Padang and Ceylon and Malaysia. The catalyst of Yankee ingenuity transformed whalebone and rattan and the hides of Indian water buffalo into an industry that encompassed more than forty factories of varying sizes and carried the economy of a sizable town on its reluctant payrolls.

In its 300th year Westfield is, in a sense, more truly than ever The Whip City. Nowhere else in the world can traditional Westfield whips be made. Nowhere else in the world is there the indigenous machinery or the skill essential to putting together a traditional Westfield driving or riding or stock-handling whip.

Let's make one distinction clear. Braided leather whips — bull-whips — can be made anywhere by anybody. They require only strips of leather and the patience to plait them. These are made in Westfield, too, but they are not truly part of the traditional Westfield industry.

A Westfield whip is made with a center of machined rawhide encased in meticulously fitted strips of rattan. It is shaped to the proper degree of flexibility and strength and covered with tough, hard-finished thread. A true Westfield whip can be made nowhere in the world except in Westfield and there only by the Westfield Whip Manufacturing Company.

This age of synthetics, naturally, has had a marked impact on the whip industry. We use fiberglas now, and nylon. This year, to provide toy whips for thousands of youngsters, we'll probably use wooden dowels and large amounts of rayon. Nevertheless, for the still substantial trade that demands the best, we make hundreds of gross of traditional Westfield whips.

Sadly, the day of the whalebone whip is gone. The whalebone, beautifully finished with gold or silver ferrules and handwoven name, was the true aristocrat of driving whips. Its name, though, was a misnomer. The material that formed the center was not bone but baleen, a tough, springly material that grows in sheets inside the whale's mouth and strains its huge intake of food.

Processing whalebone is a lost art. The baleen was soaked and softened until it was workable, cut into thin strips with a special two-handed knife, warmed and straightened over a kerosene flame. The process is still known but the skill is lost. In the early fifties an English company made a brief splurge with whalebone jockey bats but the bone was brittle and Leviathan's role in the whip industry ended, probably forever. The most cogent reason it will not be revived is that it would be unprofitable.

But all the glamour is not gone. Heavy rawhide whip centers are still made from the hides of Indian water buffalo, purchased in Pakistan, shipped from Karachi to New York and processed in little Southfield, Massachusetts, on the Connecticut border.

The rattans which form the siding are grown only on a few small Indonesian islands and transported to Hong Kong, often in junks and sometimes as contraband. In sprawling Hong Kong godowns the rattans are selected for quality, the outside skin, called slab, is removed and the core, or reed, is cut to the precise lengths and diameters specified by the Westfield Whip Manufacturing Company.

The hides, meanwhile are being prepared at the Turner & Cook plant in Southfield, as they have been for the past 70 years. The dry skins are soaked and swell to incredible thickness before being sliced into strips of the proper proportions by master knifemen in a wet and slippery cutting room. Then the heavy strips are tautened and twisted repeatedly as they dry on unique curing beds in a procedure that continues for days. Finally, they are ground and tapered to close tolerances between massive stone wheels operated on the same cam-regulated principle used in tapering whips.

It is a far-out digression but an interesting commentary on the toughness of rawhide to mention that it is rawhide, not hardware, that holds together the Mormon Tabernacle in Salt Lake City. No nails were used in building the fabled Tabernacle. Beams were bound with wet rawhide and as the untanned leather dried it compressed and indented the wood.

Finished rawhide is delivered to the Westfield Whip Mfg. Company in lengths varying from eighteen inches to six feet and in diameters ranging from straight 3/16 inch "strings" to tapered "Jumbo" centers, one-half inch thick at the heavy end and precisely ground to an eighth-inch tip. Each diameter and each length makes a specific type of whip for which the half-inch round rattan reeds must be split and shaped precisely. The siding must fit the rawhide center exactly, leaving no air space.

To accomplish this, the reeds are run first through a "splitter" which divides them lengthwise, then through a "ripper" which shaves the flat side of each half-round piece and tapers one end. The machines are simple but to produce usable siding requires precision and experience. The same process is used to make "chinks", short pieces of siding used to fill out the butt end or, to say it another way, give size to the handle end of the whip.

Rawhide centers and rattan siding are brought together at the stocking bench where they are bonded to form the interior of the whip. Originally the term for this operation was "stalking", or making whip stalks, but over the years "stock" and "stocking" came into more general use.

If the whip is to be worth making, the stocker must have the skill that comes only with experience. Since it was founded in 1946, the Westfield Whip Mfg. Co. has had Emil Grubert in charge of this essential operation. Mr. Grubert dates back to the halcyon days of the industry (1904) when the New England Whip Company was turning out many thousands of gross of whips a year. Even in those steam-powered days when whip production was at its incredible peak, he was acknowledged to be the foremost practitioner of his demanding trade.

Working at a long vat of hot glue and using only a small, four-sided brass guide the stocker slides four long and four short pieces of siding into position around the rawhide core and fastens them lightly with string. He does it with deceptive finesse. The beginner invariably winds up with a slippery handful of siding, a missing length of rawhide and glue in his hair.

The stocker tosses the new made stock to his helper, the "roper", who, using a revolving wheel, binds it firmly with cotton rope from end to end in coils about an inch apart. Stacked butt down to permit the excess glue to drain, the tightly bound stocks dry and harden for twenty-four hours.

Thoroughly dry, the stiff and clumsy-looking stocks are ready for the "rounder", an ingenious gadget devised in the Civil War era by

Liverus Hull, a prodigiously inventive mechanic who, with his father, Hiram, brought mass production to whipmaking long before Detroit made the term a household word.

The cutting component of the rounder is a set of two opposing drums about eight inches in diameter, each fitted with approximately 60 case-hardened steel knives. The drums, responding to the control of a cam regulated by a wheel-shaped device, close on the stock as it revolves between and past them horizontally, cutting smoothly but more deeply from butt to tip. After two passes through a rounder set by a skilled operator the stock has been transformed into the perfectly symmetrical shape of a quality whip.

Again the key word is "skilled." To manipulate the keys on the wheel that regulates the cam requires judgment and delicate touch but, most of all, experience. An unskilled or untalented operator may turn out whips with all the flexibility of a club or the resiliency of a length of rope.

Here again the Westfield Whip Mfg. Co. has been extremely fortunate. Ed Chojnowski, an extremely talented mechanic who joined the company in 1948, manages the factory and supervises the rounder. Ed is one of the few whipmakers of this or any other era who can make a whip from start to finish and do it perfectly. As the whip business became mechanized, everyone in it became a specialist in some particular phase of production. Ed knows it all, from start to finish, and probably knows it better than anyone else ever did.

When the stocks are "rounded", or tapered, the basement work is done and the centers are taken to the upper floor where braiding machines, traditionally called "plaiters" and later "platters" in the whip shops, apply the outer casing of thread.

Originally, the thread covering was applied by pulling a lathe-tapered stock upward vertically through the center of a barrel while a busy operator threw weighted threads transversely around it. Then braiders, developed in Europe at the tag end of the Industrial Revolution, were adapted to whipmaking and became indispensably part of it.

Here again skill and experience make the difference. A top-flight braider operator can not only ensure production and quality but can also add strength to the whip and develop amazing versatility in design. Mrs. Regina Boyle, whose domain is the bank of braiders at Westfield Whip, has watched the development and improvement of braiding machines since she first went to work in the Cargill & Cook Whip factory 62 years ago. She has found uses for them that no design engineer ever contemplated.

When the thread cover has been applied, the whips are sized lightly in a bath of warm thin glue and placed in a drying booth overnight. Next day they are rolled smooth in another ingenious machine peculiar to whipmaking and given a light coat of varnish. The final decorative touches, ferrules or "buttons" are applied, the snaps or lashes are attached to the loop ends and the whips are ready for shipment.

One important procedure which has not been mentioned in this abbreviated description of the whipmaking process is straightening. From the time they leave the rounder, whips must be straightened between each successive operation to counteract the warping effect either of moisture on rawhide or variance in the porosity of individual pieces of siding.

This is the process as it exists today. In the past twenty-five years we have discarded many time-consuming and unnecessary operations which had agglomerated in the preceding century. For example, old-time management considered hard-finished, premium thread too expensive. They used soft, run of the mill yarn and spent long and exasperating days filling the exteriors of the almost finished whips with an oil paste, tumbling them in rotating barrels, rubbing them smooth by hand, enameling them the desired color and finally varnishing them before shipment.

The process involved manpower which would make the cost prohibitive today; it was long and arduous at best and impossible in hot sultry weather. It was by discarding or improving such time and manpower-consuming operations that the Westfield Whip Manufacturing Company survived while its four competitors of 1948 — the Cargill-Cleveland Company, New England Whip Company, Windsor Whip Company of Windsor, New York, and the Duggan Whip Mfg. Company of Quincy — one by one took their places alongside the overshadowing ghosts of the original American Whip Co., U. S. Whip, the Van Deusen Co. and the other giants of the whip industry's fascinating but nebulous history.

As far into the future as anyone can foresee there will always be a demand for Westfield whips — a demand ranging, perhaps, from small to tiny but a demand nevertheless. While the demand remains the Westfield Whip Mfg. Co. will remain and Westfield will remain the Whip City of the World.

Appendix E
Excerpts from Main and Winchester Saddlery Catalog

M. & W. SNAKE WHIPS.

Arizona, California, New York, Kier.

ARIZONA—7 Feet, Weight 2¼ lbs, 1 inch at Butt, Oiled Tanned Latigo Leather, Buck Thong Stitched, 4½ feet Shot Loaded, Double Cover, Twisted Buck Point, Wire Wound Handle 3 inch and Leather Head Button. The size is carried well down to balance when hung over the shoulders.   Per dozen...... $30 00

CALIFORNIA—6 Feet, Weight 2 lbs, ⅞ inch at Butt, Oiled Tanned Latigo Leather, Buck Thong Stitched, 3 feet Flattened Bullet Loaded, Double Cover, Twisted Buck Point, Wire Wound Handle 2 inch and Leather Head Button.   The size is carried well down to balance when hung over the shoulders.   Per dozen...... $30 00

NEW YORK—6 Feet, Weight 1½ lbs, ¾ inch at Butt, Oiled Tanned Latigo Leather, Buck Thong Stitched, 3 feet Flattened Bullet Loaded, Double Cover, Twisted Buck Point, Wire Wound Handle 1¾ inch and Leather Head Button.   A Finely Finished Slim Snake.   Per dozen...... $30 00

KIER—6½ Feet, Weight 2 lbs, ¾ inch Butt, Oiled Tanned Latigo Leather, Buck Thong Stitched, Flattened Bullet Loaded from Butt to Point, Double Cover, Twisted Buck Point with extra wide Popper Sewed into Snake, Wire Wound Handle 2 inch and Leather Head Button.   Per dozen...... $48 00

JOE MEHN—7 Feet, Weight 1½ lbs, ¾ inch Butt, Oiled Tanned Latigo Leather, Buck Thong Stitched, Flattened Bullet Loaded from Butt to Point, Double Cover, Twisted Buck Point with a Loop in the center of the Point, the Point is sewed into the end of the Snake, Wire Wound Handle 1½ inch and Leather Head Button.   Per dozen...... $42 00

No. X X X, Sacramento, M. & W. Extra Heavy.

No. X X X.—6 Feet, Weight 1½ lbs, 1 inch at Butt, Oiled Tanned Latigo Leather, Buck Thong Stitched, Flattened Bullet Loaded Butt, Double Cover, Twisted Buck Point, Wire Wound Handle 6 inch and Two Leather Buttons.   Per dozen...... $20 00

SACRAMENTO—6 Feet, Weight 2 lbs, ⅞ inch at Butt, Oiled Tanned Latigo Leather, Buck Thong Stitched, 3½ feet Flattened Bullet Loaded Butt, Double Cover, Twisted Buck Point, Wire Wound Handle 6 inch and Two Leather Buttons.   Per dozen...... $48 00

M. & W. EXTRA HEAVY—7 Feet, Weight 4 lbs, 1 inch at Butt, Oiled Tanned Latigo Leather, Buck Thong Stitched, Flattened Bullet Loaded from Butt to Point, Double Cover, Twisted Buck Point Sewed into the Snake, Wire Wound Handle 6 inch and Two Leather Buttons.   Per dozen...... $60 00

Leadville.

LEADVILLE—7½ Feet. Weight 2¼ lbs, 1 inch at Butt, Oiled Tanned Latigo Leather, Buck Thong Stitched, 4½ feet Shot Loaded, Double Cover, 8 Plait Braided Buck Point 3 feet Long, Turk's Head End to Butt.   Per dozen...... $60 00

Montana.

MONTANA—6 Feet, Weight 2 lbs, 1 inch at Butt, Oiled Tanned Latigo Leather, Buck Thong Stitched, 3½ feet Shot Loaded, Double Cover, 8 Plait Braided Buck Point 2½ feet Long, Plain Finished End.   Per dozen...... $36 00

Eureka.

EUREKA—6 Feet, Weight 1¼ lbs, ⅞ inch at Butt, Oiled Tanned Latigo Leather, Buck Thong Stitched, 2½ feet Shot Loaded, Double Cover, 4 Plait Braided Buck Point 12 inches long, Turk's Head End.   Per dozen...... $24 00

SNAKE WHIPS.

No. O. X.

Io. O. X.—6 Feet, Weight 1½ lbs, 1½ inch at Butt, Oiled Tanned Latigo Leather, Buck Thong Stitched, 3 feet
Shot Loaded, Double Cover, 4 Plait Braided Buck Point 12 inches long, Two Leather Buttons and Wrist Loop.
                                                                                Per dozen....... $24 00

No. X. L.

Io. X. L.—6 Feet, Weight 1½ lbs, 1 inch at Butt, Oiled Tanned Latigo Leather, Buck Thong Stitched, Flattened
Bullet Loaded Butt, Double Cover, Twisted Buck Point, Two Leather Buttons.   Per dozen $21 00

Braided Snake.

BRAIDED SNAKE—5½ Feet, Weight 1½ lbs, ½ inch at Butt, 16 Plait Solid Buckskin, 3 Feet Shot Loaded,
Fine Turk's Head Finish.   Per dozen...... $60 00

No. X.

No. X.—6 Feet, 1½ inch Butt, Oiled Tanned Latigo Leather, Buck Thong Stitched, Twisted Buck Point, Two
Braided Head Buttons.   Per dozen...... $18 00

No. O.

No. O.—5 Feet, 1½ inch Butt, Oiled Tanned Latigo Leather, Buck Thong Stitched, Twisted Buck Point, Two
Braided Head Buttons.   Per dozen...... $15 00

Acme.

ACME—5 Feet, 1 inch Butt Loaded, Oiled Tanned Latigo Leather, Buck Thong Stitched, Braided 4 Plait Point 2½
feet long, Wrist Loop.   Per dozen...... $13 00

Encore.

ENCORE—5 Feet, 1 inch Butt Loaded, Leather Center, 2½ foot Braided 4 Plait Point, Thread Plaited Stock, Braided
Head Button with Wrist Loop.   Per dozen...... $9 00

A WORD IN REGARD TO SNAKE WHIPS.

We have been making these goods right here in San Francisco since the days of '49, and come into closer touch with the man who
carries the whip than any Eastern manufacturer. *We study his wants.* His opinion carries weight as none other can, and in
Flexibility, Swing, Finish and *Durability* we furnish the Snake par excellence. We tan the leather in our own tannery from choice
plump heifer hides, there is nothing better. The stitch on the cheapest to the best is always Buckskin and sewed by hand. The
loading is done with great care and our Snakes will correspond exactly to weights given under each grade. We are in a position to
make to order any Special Goods in this line and can guarantee satisfaction. Send us a sample, we will duplicate it, or give a full
description if sample is not to be had.   E

STOCK WHIPS.

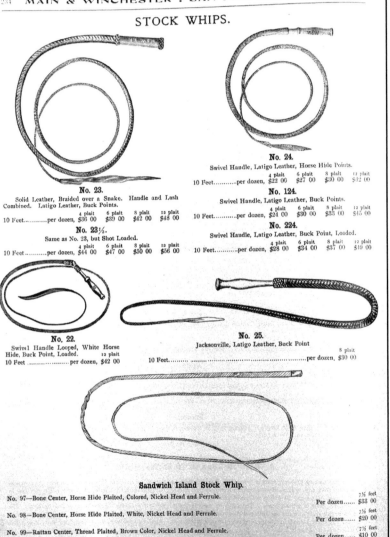

No. 24.
Swivel Handle, Latigo Leather, Horse Hide Points.

	4 plait	6 plait	8 plait	12 plait
10 Feet..........per dozen,	$22 00	$27 00	$30 00	$42 00

No. 23.
Solid Leather, Braided over a Snake. Handle and Lash Combined. Latigo Leather, Buck Points.

	4 plait	6 plait	8 plait	12 plait
10 Feet...........per dozen,	$36 00	$39 00	$42 00	$48 00

No. 23½.
Same as No. 23, but Shot Loaded.

	4 plait	6 plait	8 plait	12 plait
10 Feet ....per dozen,	$44 00	$47 00	$50 00	$56 00

No. 124.
Swivel Handle, Latigo Leather, Buck Points.

	4 plait	6 plait	8 plait	12 plait
10 Feet...........per dozen,	$24 00	$30 00	$33 00	$45 00

No. 224.
Swivel Handle, Latigo Leather, Buck Point, Loaded.

	4 plait	6 plait	8 plait	12 plait
10 Feet...........per dozen,	$28 00	$34 00	$37 00	$49 00

No. 22.
Swivel Handle Looped, White Horse Hide, Buck Point, Loaded.

	12 plait
10 Feet ....per dozen,	$42 00

No. 25.
Jacksonville, Latigo Leather, Buck Point

	8 plait
10 Feet................ ....per dozen,	$30 00

Sandwich Island Stock Whip.

No. 97—Bone Center, Horse Hide Plaited, Colored, Nickel Head and Ferrule.
7½ feet
Per dozen...... $33 00

No. 98—Bone Center, Horse Hide Plaited, White, Nickel Head and Ferrule.
7½ feet
Per dozen...... $20 00

No. 99—Rattan Center, Thread Plaited, Brown Color, Nickel Head and Ferrule.
7½ feet
Per dozen...... $10 00

WHIP STOCKS.

No. 1 M & W. Hickory.

Our No. 1 M. & W. Hickory Stocks are Hickory. They are hand shaved. The Keepers with a black Linen Thread. Each Stock is marked and when so marked are guaranteed.

MAIN
&
WINCHESTER
XX HICKORY
San Francisco
Cal.

made from the straightest second growth White are heavy Buckskin, put on in our own factory on the butt, as shown in the cut, with our name.

Length, 4 feet 4½ feet 5 feet 5½ feet 6 feet
Per dozen..... $5 00 $6 00 $7 00 $8 00 $9 00

No. 2 M. & W. Hickory.

The No. 2 M. & W. Hickory Stocks are the second selection from the No. 1, and do not have our name on them. They are White Hickory, equal to the No. 1 ordinarily sold.

Length, 4 feet 4½ feet 5 feet
Per dozen..... $3 50 $4 00 $4 50

No. 3 Hickory Stocks.

White with Buckskin Keepers.

Length, 4 feet 4½ feet 5 feet
Per dozen..... $2 20 $2 50 $3 00

No. 1 M. & W. Hickory with 7 Ferrules.

No. 1—7 Ferrules. Nickel.

Length, 4 feet 4½ feet 5 feet
Per dozen..... $7 00 $8 00 $9 00

No. 1 M. & W. Hickory with 7 Ferrules and Leather Handle.

No. 1—Nickel Head and 7 Ferrules, Russet Coltskin Leather Handle.

Length, 4 feet 4½ feet 5 feet
Per dozen...... $9 00 $10 00 $11 00

Malacca Stocks.

Natural Malacca, 1½ inch, Nickel Head and Ferrules, Buckskin Keepers.

Length, 4 feet 4½ feet 5 feet 5½ feet 6 feet
Per dozen...... $8 00 $9 00 $10 00 $12 00 $15 00

Two-Thirds Bone, Covered and Ferruled.

Two-Third Bone, Full Stocked, Loaded Butt, Black Thread Covered, 1½ inch Nickel Head and nine 1½ inch Nickel Ferrules; Buckskin Keep.

4½ feet
Per dozen...... $36 00

Bare Bone Whip Stocks.

Polished and Oiled Hickory Handle. Heavy Bone from Handle to Tip. The center is Thread Plaited with 23 Nickel Ferrules; the top is Bare Bone 18 inches, Buckskin Keeper, Thread wound with Two Thread Hand Plaited Buttons.

4½ feet
Each...... $12 00 to $15 00. **E**

LASHES.

All Lashes quoted below are made in our own factory in San Francisco.

The Buckskin used in them is the finest selection of Oil Tanned California skins. The fact that they are all **Hand Plaited** insures the consumer an article that is perfect in workmanship and far superior in durability to the machine plaited lashes that are offered to the trade by many jobbers.

The Extra Quality and No. 1 Solid Buckskin Lashes are buckskin plaited and buckskin filler. The No. 1 being made in two sizes for Stage, light, and for Team, heavy. We can furnish to order any length or number of plait of lashes in all the grades quoted below and pay particular attention to the demands of those requiring special lashes for Harvester or any other purpose.

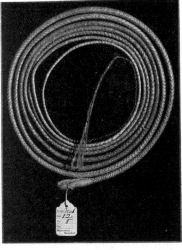

Lashes sent to us to be retipped will be promptly attended to and returned to sender by mail. This being the quickest and cheapest transportation for small quantities. When sending in such lashes state plainly who they are from and postoffice address and how many feet in length each separate lash is to be when retipped.

Main & Winchester lashes go to the entire length of the Pacific Coast and Middle West and the reputation established on them is the envy and dismay of all competitors.

Buy them and you are **assured of good goods and pleased** customers.

M. & W. LASHES.

Extra Quality, Solid Buckskin, Stage.

		6 plait	8 plait	12 plait	16 plait
10 Feet	per dozen,	$30 00	$36 00	$48 00	$60 00
12 Feet	"	36 00	42 00	60 00	72 00
16 Feet	"	48 00	60 00	72 00	96 00

No. 1 Solid Buckskin, Stage or Team.

		4 plait	6 plait	8 plait	12 plait	16 plait
6 Feet	per dozen,	$12 00	$15 00	$17 00	$20 00	$......
10 Feet	"	20 00	25 00	27 00	30 00	48 00
12 Feet	"	24 00	30 00	33 00	42 00	60 00
16 Feet	"	33 00	36 00	42 00	54 00	78 00

No. 2 Buckskin, Team.

		4 plait	6 plait	8 plait	12 plait
6 Feet	per dozen,	$ 9 00	$10 00	$12 00	$......
10 Feet	"	14 00	16 50	18 00	24 00
12 Feet	"	17 00	20 00	24 00	27 50
16 Feet	"	24 00	27 00	30 00	36 00

No. 1 Horse Hide, Buck Tip.

		4 plait	6 plait	8 plait
6 Feet	per dozen,	$ 7 00	$ 9 00	$......
10 Feet	"	12 00	15 00	18 00
12 Feet	"	15 00	18 00	21 00
16 Feet	"	21 00	27 00	30 00

No. 2 Horse Hide.

		4 plait	6 plait	8 plait
4 to 5 Feet	per dozen,	$ 3 00	$......	$......
6 Feet	"	6 00	7 50	10 00
10 Feet	"	9 00	13 00	16 00
12 Feet	"	12 00	15 00	20 00
16 Feet	"	16 00	21 00	27 00

Thread Lashes.

	6 feet	10 feet	12 feet	16 feet.
Per dozen	$4 00	$7 00	$8 00	$12 00

E

Appendix F
Diamond Whip Co. Catalog

TO THE BUYER

Dear Sir:

We call your attention to the various merchandise in this descriptive and illustrated catalog, and guarantee every article will give satisfaction, and if for any reason any article should not mark up to the standard by some slight defect overlooked in the final inspection, we will deem it a favor on your part to tell us about it and give us an opportunity to rectify it.

Any of our goods returned to us charges prepaid will be repaired and put in first-class condition free of charge, unless the article shows abuse or long use. Then we would only make a very nominal charge.

Our many years of experience in this line of business has enabled us to offer you the very highest standard attained in workmanship and finish. We are proud to make this assertion, that our factory is the best equipped in the United States and we employ the most efficient workmen obtainable.

We use nothing but the highest grade of leather in the manufacture of our merchandise. Good leather is the effect of good tanning. We tan all our own leather, which enables us to know that it is properly prepared. Properly tanned leather gives it strength and durability. Long wear is the keynote of our merchandise.

Particular attention is called to the different lengths of our whips. We guarantee our whips and lashes to be full length without measuring the loop and snap, while other manufacturers measure the loop and snap in selling the different lengths of whips and lashes. Also, we wish to call attention to our whips Nos. 400, 503, 504, 506, 508 and 524, which are 6-plait the entire length, while others braid but a short distance 6-plait and the balance 4-plait, which does not give the whips the proper swing or wear, and you are charged for a 6-plait whip.

We want you to become one of our regular customers and would kindly ask you to favor us with a trial order. Then you will learn that you can always save money and get good merchandise of guaranteed quality from the DIAMOND WHIP CO.

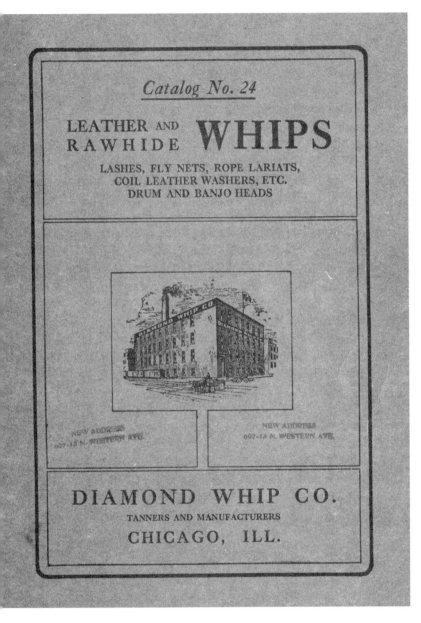

Catalog No. 24

LEATHER AND WHIPS
RAWHIDE

LASHES, FLY NETS, ROPE LARIATS,
COIL LEATHER WASHERS, ETC.
DRUM AND BANJO HEADS

NEW ADDRESS
607-13 N. WESTERN AVE.

NEW ADDRESS
607-13 N. WESTERN AVE.

DIAMOND WHIP CO.
TANNERS AND MANUFACTURERS
CHICAGO, ILL.

Cattle Whips

350 Equipped with our **Patented Tip Top Nickel Revolving Handle.** Strongest and easiest revolving handle ever made. Equaled by none. 8 Plait Russet Latigo Calf Leather, Solid Leather Center, White Buck Point, 2 Leather Buttons and Buck Snap.

	6 ft.	8 ft.	10 ft.	12 ft.	14 ft.
Per dozen	$30.00	$32.25	$34.50	$35.25	$37.50

352 Same as above in **Shot Loaded.**

Per dozen					

358 Equipped with our **Patented Tip Top Nickel Revolving Handle.** Strongest and easiest revolving handle ever made. Equaled by none. 12 Plait Russet Latigo Calf Leather, Solid Leather Center, White Buck Point, 2 Leather Buttons and Buck Snap.

	10 ft.	12 ft.	14 ft.
Per dozen			

360 Same as above in **Shot Loaded.**

	10 ft.	12 ft.	14 ft.
Per dozen			

Cattle Whips—continued

362 Equipped with our **Patented Tip Top Nickel Revolving Handle.** Strongest and easiest revolving handle ever made. Equaled by none. 8 Plait Russet Latigo Calf Leather, White Leather Interlaced at Handle, Solid Leather Center, White Buck Point, 2 Leather Buttons and Buck Snap.

	6 ft.	8 ft.	10 ft.	12 ft.	14 ft.
Per dozen					

364 Same as above in **Shot Loaded.**

Per dozen					

374 Equipped with our **Patented Tip Top Nickel Revolving Handle.** Strongest and easiest revolving handle ever made. Equaled by none. 12 Plait Heavy Black Upper Shoe Leather, Solid Leather Center, White Buck Point, 2 Leather Buttons and Buck Snap.

	10 ft.	12 ft.	14 ft.
Per dozen			

376 Same as above in **Shot Loaded.**

	10 ft.	12 ft.	14 ft.
Per dozen			

Cattle Whips-continued

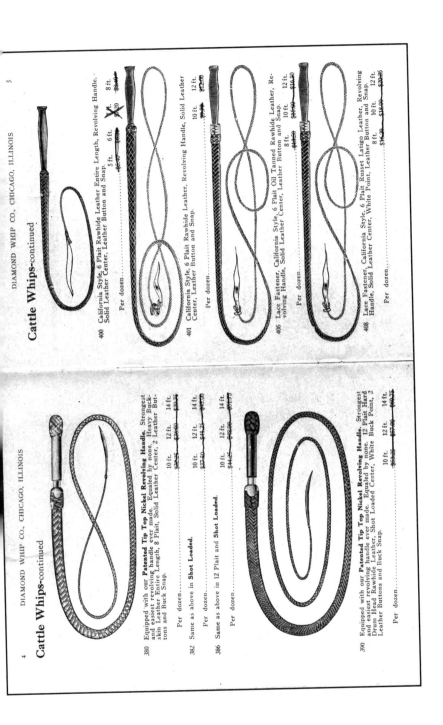

400 California Style, 6 Plait Rawhide Leather Entire Length, Revolving Handle. Solid Leather Center, Leather Button and Snap.

5 ft.   6 ft.   8 ft.

Per dozen..........

401 California Style, 6 Plait Rawhide Leather, Revolving Handle, Solid Leather Center, Leather Button and Snap.

10 ft.   12 ft.

Per dozen..........

406 Lace Fastener, California Style, 6 Plait Oil Tanned Rawhide Leather, Revolving Handle, Solid Leather Center, Leather Button and Snap.

8 ft.   10 ft.   12 ft.

Per dozen..........

408 Lace Fastener, California Style, 6 Plait Russet Latigo Leather, Revolving Handle, Solid Leather Center, White Point, Leather Button and Snap.

8 ft.   10 ft.   12 ft.

Per dozen..........

Cattle Whips-continued

380 Equipped with our **Patented Tip Top Nickel Revolving Handle. Strongest and easiest revolving handle ever made.** Equaled by none. Heavy Buckskin Leather Entire Length, 8 Plait, Solid Leather Center, 2 Leather Buttons and Buck Snap.

10 ft.   12 ft.   14 ft.

Per dozen..........

382 Same as above in **Shot Loaded.**

10 ft.   12 ft.   14 ft.

Per dozen..........

386 Same as above in 12 Plait and **Shot Loaded.**

10 ft.   12 ft.   14 ft.

Per dozen..........

390 Equipped with our **Patented Tip Top Nickel Revolving Handle. Strongest and easiest revolving handle ever made.** Equaled by none. 12 Plait Hard Drum Head Rawhide Leather, Shot Loaded Center, White Buck Point, 2 Leather Buttons and Buck Snap.

10 ft.   12 ft.   14 ft.

Per dozen..........

Appendix F

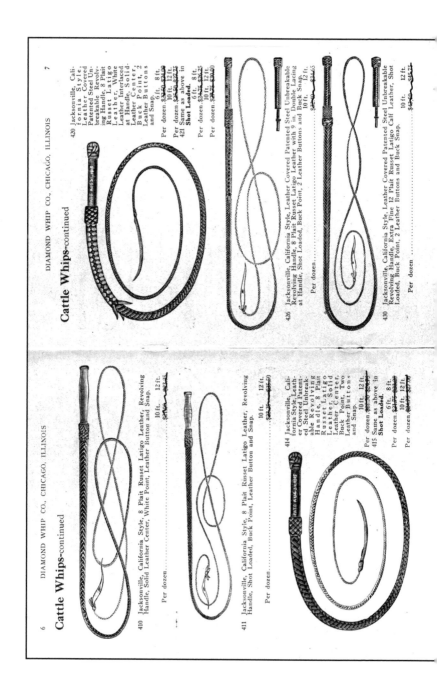

Cattle Whips-continued

410 Jacksonville, California Style, 8 Plait Russet Latigo Leather, Revolving Handle, Solid Leather Center, White Point, Leather Button and Snap.

10 ft. 12 ft.

Per dozen..................

411 Jacksonville, California Style, 8 Plait Russet Latigo Leather, Revolving Handle, Shot Loaded, Buck Point, Leather Button and Snap.

10 ft. 12 ft.

Per dozen..................

414 Jacksonville, California Style, Leather Covered Patented Steel Unbreakable Revolving Handle, 8 Plait Russet Latigo Leather, Solid Leather Center, Buck Point, Two Leather Buttons and Snap.

10 ft. 12 ft.

Per dozen..................

415 Same as above in **Shot Loaded.**

6 ft. 8 ft.

Per dozen..................

10 ft. 12 ft.

Per dozen..................

Cattle Whips-continued

420 Jacksonville, California Style, Leather Covered Patented Steel Unbreakable Revolving Handle, 8 Plait Russet Latigo Leather, White Leather Interlaced at Handle, Solid Leather Center, Buck Point, 2 Leather Buttons and Snap.

6 ft. 8 ft.

Per dozen..................

10 ft. 12 ft.

421 Same as above in **Shot Loaded.**

6 ft. 8 ft.

10 ft. 12 ft.

Per dozen..................

426 Jacksonville, California Style, Leather Covered Patented Steel Unbreakable Revolving Handle, 8 Plait Russet Latigo Leather with 9 in. Double Lacing at Handle, Shot Loaded, Buck Point, 2 Leather Buttons and Back Snap.

Per dozen..................

430 Jacksonville, California Style, Leather Covered Patented Steel Unbreakable Revolving Handle, Extra Fine 12 Plait Russet Latigo Calf Leather, Shot Loaded, Buck Point, 2 Leather Buttons and Back Snap.

10 ft. 12 ft.

Per dozen..................

DIAMOND WHIP CO., CHICAGO, ILLINOIS

Solid Leather Team Whips

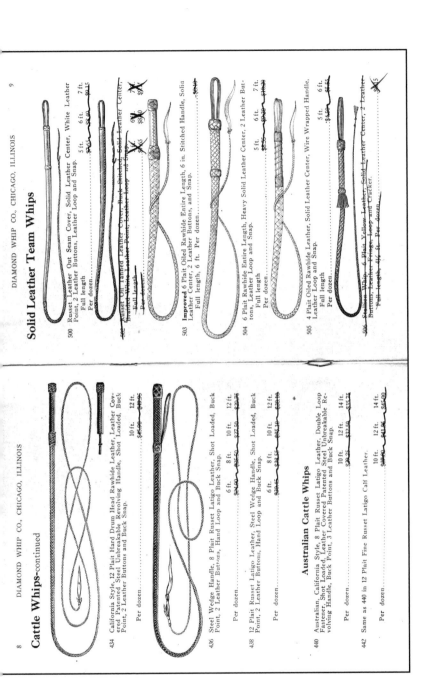

500 Russet Leather Out Seam Cover, Solid Leather Center, White Leather Point, 2 Leather Buttons, Leather Loop and Snap.

Full length	5 ft.	6 ft.	7 ft.
Per dozen	$7.65	$8.40	$9.15

501 Russet Oil Tanned Leather Cover, Back Stitched, Solid Leather Center, Braided White Leather Point, Leather Loop and Snap.

Full length	5 ft.	6 ft.	7 ft.
Per dozen	$75	$90	$9

503 Improved 6 Plait Oiled Rawhide Entire Length, 6 in. Stitched Handle, Solid Leather Center, 2 Leather Buttons, and Snap.
Full length, 6 ft. Per dozen.... $9.40

504 6 Plait Rawhide Entire Length, Heavy Solid Leather Center, 2 Leather Buttons, Leather Loop and Snap.

Full length	5 ft.	6 ft.	7 ft.
Per dozen	$5.55	$7.20	$7.85

505 4 Plait Oiled Rawhide Leather, Solid Leather Center, Wire Wrapped Handle, Leather Loop and Snap.

Full length	5 ft.	6 ft.
Per dozen	$7.80	$8.55

506 Scottish Whip, 6 Plait Yellow Leather, Solid Leather Center, 2 Leather Buttons, Leather Fringe Loop and Cracker.
Full length, 4½ ft. Per dozen.... $45

Cattle Whips-continued

434 California Style, 12 Plait Hard Drum Head Rawhide Leather, Leather Covered Patented Steel Unbreakable Revolving Handle, Shot Loaded, Buck Point, 2 Leather Buttons and Buck Snap.

	10 ft.	12 ft.
Per dozen	$45.00	$49.95

436 Steel Wedge Handle, 8 Plait Russet Latigo Leather, Shot Loaded, Buck Point, 2 Leather Buttons, Hand Loop and Buck Snap.

	6 ft.	8 ft.	10 ft.	12 ft.
Per dozen	$24.00	$25.50	$27.50	$29.25

438 12 Plait Russet Latigo Leather, Steel Wedge Handle, Shot Loaded, Buck Point, 2 Leather Buttons, Hand Loop and Buck Snap.

	6 ft.	8 ft.	10 ft.	12 ft.
Per dozen	$29.45	$32.45	$35.40	$38.40

Australian Cattle Whips

440 Australian, California Style, 8 Plait Russet Latigo Leather, Double Loop Fastener, Shot Loaded, Leather Covered Patented Steel Unbreakable Revolving Handle, Buck Point, 3 Leather Buttons and Buck Snap.

	10 ft.	12 ft.	14 ft.
Per dozen	$9.25	$12.50	$15.25

442 Same as 440 in 12 Plait Fine Russet Latigo Calf Leather.

	10 ft.	12 ft.	14 ft.
Per dozen	$37.50	$41.95	$45.00

Solid Leather Team Whips-continued

508   XXXX Heavy Solid Leather Wagon Whip, 6 Plait Patented Diamond Hard Drum Rawhide Through to Snap, 2 Wide Leather Buttons with Brass Nails, Leather Loop and Snap.

Full length

	5 ft.	6 ft.	7 ft.
Per dozen......	$9.75	$12.15	$14.70

510   XX Russet Oil Tanned Leather, Buck Stitched, Solid Leather Center, 2 Leather Buttons Fastened with Brass Headed Nails, 12 in. Braided Buck Point, Leather Loop and Snap.

	4 ft.	4½ ft.	5 ft.	5½ ft.	6 ft.
Buck Stitched Cover					
Per dozen......	$10.35	$11.55	$12.75	$14.10	$15.45

512   XXXX Best Russet Oil Tanned Leather, Extra Qua'ity, Buck Stitched, Solid Leather Center, 2 Extra Wide Leather Buttons Fastened with Brass Headed Nails, 12 in. Braided Buck Point, Leather Loop and Snap.

	4 ft.	4½ ft.	5 ft.	5½ ft.	6 ft.
Buck Stitched Cover					
Per dozen......	$12.00	$13.50	$15.00	$16.50	$18.00

Express Whips

514   Russet Leather Oiled Cover, Buck Stitched, Rawhide Center, White Horsehide Top, 2 Leather Buttons and Snap.

7 ft. Per dozen.. $15.90

520   Rawhide Express, Russet Leather Cover, Out Seam, 4½ ft. Stock with a Large Through Rawhide Center, 4 Plait Buck Point, Leather Button and Snap.

Full Length, 8 ft. Per dozen... $14.20

524   Rawhide Express, 6 Plait Patent Hard Drum Rawhide, 10 in. Russet Leather Buck Stitched Handle, 4½ ft. Stock with a Large Through Rawhide Center, 6 Plait Buck Point, 2 Fine Leather Buttons and Buck Snap.

Per dozen, 7 ft.........................$18.00   Per dozen, 8 ft..................................$20.25

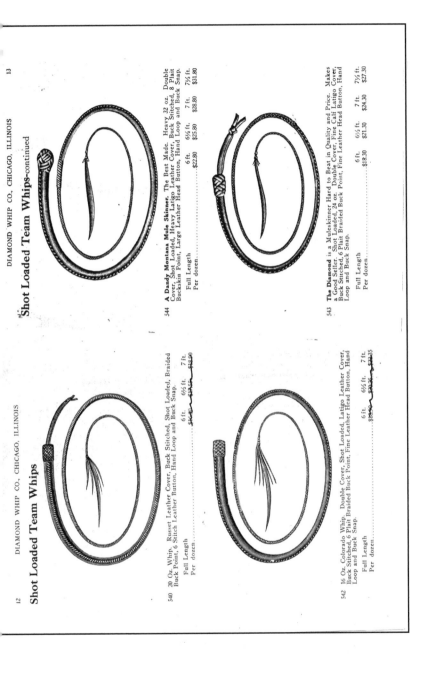

Shot Loaded Team Whips

540 20 Oz. Whip. Russet Leather Cover, Buck Stitched, Shot Loaded, Braided Buck Point, 6 Stitch Leather Button, Hand Loop and Buck Snap.

	6 ft.	6½ ft.	7 ft.
Full Length			
Per dozen	$16.80	$18.30	$19.80

542 16 Oz. Colorado Whip. Double Cover, Shot Loaded, Latigo Leather Cover, Buck Stitched, 6 Plait Braided Buck Point, Fine Leather Head Button, Hand Loop and Buck Snap.

	6 ft.	6½ ft.	7 ft.
Full Length			
Per dozen	$18.50	$20.35	$22.05

Shot Loaded Team Whips—continued

544 A Dandy Montana Mule Skinner. The Best Made. Heavy 32 oz. Double Cover, Shot Loaded, Heavy Latigo Leather Cover, Buck Stitched, 8 Plait Buckskin Point, Large Leather Head Button, Hand Loop and Buck Snap.

	6 ft.	6½ ft.	7 ft.	7½ ft.
Full Length				
Per dozen	$22.80	$25.80	$28.80	$31.80

543 The Diamond is a Muleskinner Hard to Beat in Quality and Price. Makes a Good Seller. Shot Loaded, 24 oz. Double Cover, Fine Calf Latigo Cover, Buck Stitched, 6 Plait Braided Buck Point, Fine Leather Head Button, Hand Loop and Buck Snap.

	6 ft.	6½ ft.	7 ft.	7½ ft.
Full Length				
Per dozen	$18.30	$21.30	$24.30	$27.30

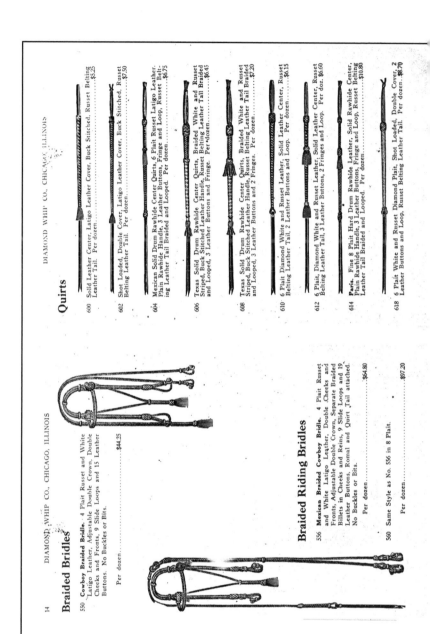

Quirts

600 Solid Leather Center, Latigo Leather Cover, Buck Stitched, Russet Belting Leather Tail. Per dozen.......$5.25

602 Shot Loaded, Double Cover, Latigo Leather Cover, Buck Stitched, Russet Belting Leather Tail. Per dozen.......$7.50

604 Mexican Solid Drum Rawhide Center Quirts, 6 Plait Russet Latigo Leather, Plain Rawhide Handle, 3 Leather Buttons, Fringe and Loop, Russet Belting Leather Tail Braided and Looped. Per dozen.......$6.75

606 Texas Solid Drum Rawhide Center Quirts, Braided White and Russet Striped, Buck Stitched Leather Handle, Russet Belting Leather Tail Braided and Looped, 3 Leather Buttons and Fringe. Per dozen.......$6.45

608 Texas Solid Drum Rawhide Center Quirts, Braided White and Russet Striped, Buck Stitched Leather Handle, Russet Belting Leather Tail Braided and Looped, 3 Leather Buttons and 2 Fringes. Per dozen.......$7.20

610 6 Plait Diamond White and Russet Leather, Solid Leather Center, Russet Belting Leather Tail, 2 Leather Buttons and Loop. Per dozen.......$6.15

612 6 Plait, Diamond White and Russet Leather, Solid Leather Center, Russet Belting Leather Tail, 3 Leather Buttons, 2 Fringes and Loop. Per doz. $6.60

614 Paris, Fine 8 Plait Hard Drum Rawhide Leather, Solid Rawhide Center, Plain Rawhide Handle, 3 Leather Buttons, Fringe and Loop, Russet Belting Leather Tail Braided and Looped. Per dozen.......$10.80

618 6 Plait White and Russet Diamond Plait, Shot Loaded, Double Cover, 2 Leather Buttons and Loop, Russet Belting Leather Tail. Per dozen.......$8.70

Braided Bridles

550 Cowboy Braided Bridle. 4 Plait Russet and White Latigo Leather, Adjustable Double Crown, Double Cheeks and Fronts, 9 Slide Loops and 15 Leather Buttons. No Buckles or Bits.

Per dozen.......$44.25

Braided Riding Bridles

556 Mexican Braided Cowboy Bridle. 4 Plait Russet and White Latigo Leather, Double Cheeks and Fronts, Adjustable Double Crown, Separate Braided Billets in Cheeks and Reins, 9 Slide Loops and 19 Leather Buttons, Romal and Quirt Tail attached. No Buckles or Bits.

Per dozen.......$64.80

560 Same Style as No. 556 in 8 Plait.

Per dozen.......$97.20

Quirts-continued

620 6 Plait White and Russet Diamond Plait, Shot Loaded, Double Cover, 3 Leather Buttons, 2 Fringes and Loop, Russet Belting Leather Tail. Per dozen $9.45

622 8 Plait White and Russet Leather Striped, Shot Loaded, Double Cover, 2 Leather Buttons and Loop, Russet Belting Leather Tail. Per dozen... $9.75

624 **Leader.** 8 Plait, White and Russet Striped, Shot Loaded, Double Cover, 3 Leather Buttons, 2 Fringes and Loop, Russet Belting Leather Tail. Per dozen................... $10.65

626 **Native.** Fine 8 Plait Russet Latigo Leather, Shot Loaded, Double Cover, 3 Leather Buttons and Loop, Russet Belting Leather Tail. Per dozen. $13.50

628 Same style as 626 in 12 Plait. Per dozen.............. 17.55

630 Same style as 626 in 16 Plait. Per dozen.............. 24.30

632 **Western.** Fine 8 Plait Russet Latigo Leather, Shot Loaded, Double Cover, 4 Leather Buttons, 2 Fringes and Loop, Russet Belting Leather Tail. Per dozen $14.70

634 Same style as 632 in 12 Plait. Per dozen.............. 18.75

636 Same style as 632 in 16 Plait. Per dozen.............. 27.00

638 12 Plait French Calf Leather, White and Russet Striped, Shot Loaded, Double Cover, 3 Fine Leather Buttons and Loop, Russet Belting Leather Tail. Per dozen $17.55

640 **California.** 12 Plait French Calf Leather, White and Russet Striped, Shot Loaded, Double Cover, 4 Leather Buttons, 2 Fringes and Loop, Russet Belting Leather Tail. Per dozen............ $18.75

Quirts-continued

642 16 Plait French Calf Leather, White and Russet Striped with Checkered Center, Shot Loaded, Double Cover, 3 Fine Leather Buttons and Loop, Russet Belting Leather Tail. Per dozen.....$??.??

644 Extra Fine 8 Plait Transparent Hard Drum Head Rawhide Leather, Shot Loaded, Double Cover, 3 Latigo Leather Buttons and Loop, Russet Belting Leather Tail. Per dozen...............$??.??

648 Same style as 644 in 12 Plait. Per dozen........ 18.??

650 Same style as 644 in 16 Plait. Per dozen........ 27.00

652 Extra Fine 8 Plait Transparent Hard Drum Head Rawhide Leather, Shot Loaded, Double Cover, 4 Latigo Leather Buttons, 2 Fringes and Loop, Russet Belting Leather Tail. Per dozen...........$??.??

656 Same style as 652 in 12 Plait. Per dozen........ 2?.??

658 Same style as 652 in 16 Plait. Per dozen........ 2?.??

660 12 Plait Fine White French Calf Leather, Shot Loaded, Double Cover, 3 Leather Buttons and Loop, Russet Belting Leather Tail. Per dozen....$??.??

662 12 Plait Fine White French Calf Leather, Shot Loaded, Double Cover, 4 Leather Buttons, 2 Fringes and Loop, Russet Belting Leather Tail. Per dozen ....$??.??

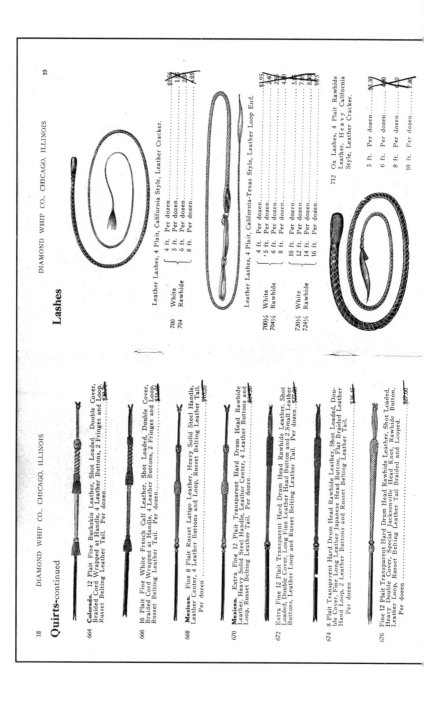

Quirts-continued

664 Colorado. 12 Plait Fine Buckskin Leather, Shot Loaded. Double Cover, Braided Cord Wrapped at Handle, 4 Leather Buttons, 2 Fringes and Loop, Russet Belting Leather Tail. Per dozen.............

666 16 Plait Fine White French Calf Leather, Shot Loaded, Double Cover, Braided Cord Wrapped at Handle, 4 Leather Buttons, 2 Fringes and Loop, Russet Belting Leather Tail. Per dozen.............

668 Mexican. Fine 8 Plait Russet Latigo Leather, Heavy Solid Steel Handle, Leather Center, 4 Leather Buttons and Loop, Russet Belting Leather Tail. Per dozen.............

670 Mexican. Extra Fine 12 Plait Transparent Hard Drum Head Rawhide Leather, Heavy Solid Steel Handle, Leather Center, 4 Leather Buttons and Loop, Russet Belting Leather Tail. Per dozen.............

672 Extra Fine 12 Plait Transparent Hard Drum Head Rawhide Leather, Shot Loaded, Double Cover, Long Fine Leather Head Button and 2 Small Leather Buttons, Leather Loop and Russet Belting Leather Tail. Per dozen.............

674 8 Plait Transparent Hard Drum Head Rawhide Leather, Shot Loaded, Double Cover, Fine Long Leather Japanese Head Button, Flat Braided Leather Hand Loop, 2 Leather Buttons and Russet Belting Leather Tail. Per dozen.............

676 Fine 12 Plait Transparent Hard Drum Head Rawhide Leather, Shot Loaded, Heavy Double Cover, Special Jacksonville Head Knot, Rawhide Button, Leather Loop, Russet Belting Leather Tail Braided and Looped. Per dozen.............

Lashes

Leather Lashes, 4 Plait, California Style, Leather Cracker.

700	White	4 ft.	Per dozen.............$1.??
		5 ft.	Per dozen............. 1.??
704	Rawhide	6 ft.	Per dozen............. 2.??
		8 ft.	Per dozen............. ??5

Leather Lashes, 4 Plait, California-Texas Style, Leather Loop End.

700½	White	4 ft.	Per dozen.............$1.95
		5 ft.	Per dozen............. ?.??
704½	Rawhide	6 ft.	Per dozen............. 2.??
		8 ft.	Per dozen............. 4.??
720½	White	10 ft.	Per dozen............. 5.??
		12 ft.	Per dozen............. 7.??
724½	Rawhide	14 ft.	Per dozen............. 8.??
		16 ft.	Per dozen............. 9.75

712 Ox Lashes, 4 Plait Rawhide Leather, Heavy California Style, Leather Cracker.

5 ft.	Per dozen.........	$3.30
6 ft.	Per dozen.........	4.00
8 ft.	Per dozen.........	6.?0
10 ft.	Per dozen.........	7.?0

Lashes-continued

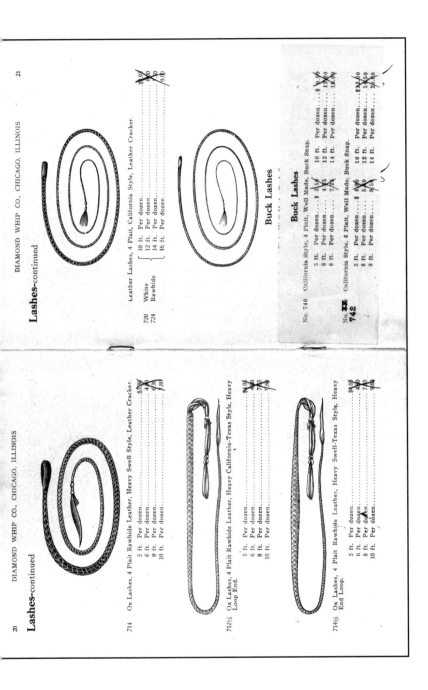

714 Ox Lashes, 4 Plait Rawhide Leather, Heavy Swell Style, Leather Cracker.

5 ft.	Per dozen	$3.90
6 ft.	Per dozen	
8 ft.	Per dozen	.70
10 ft.	Per dozen	.80

712½ Ox Lashes, 4 Plait Rawhide Leather, Heavy California-Texas Style, Heavy Loop End.

5 ft.	Per dozen	
6 ft.	Per dozen	
8 ft.	Per dozen	.75
10 ft.	Per dozen	

714½ Ox Lashes, 4 Plait Rawhide Leather, Heavy Swell-Texas Style, Heavy End Loop.

5 ft.	Per dozen	
6 ft.	Per dozen	
8 ft.	Per dozen	.75
10 ft.	Per dozen	

Lashes-continued

Leather Lashes, 4 Plait, California Style, Leather Cracker.

720	White	10 ft.	Per dozen
724	Rawhide	12 ft.	Per dozen
		14 ft.	Per dozen
		16 ft.	Per dozen $9.00

Buck Lashes

No. 740 California Style, 4 Plait, Well Made, Buck Snap.

5 ft.	Per dozen	$3.50	10 ft.	Per dozen	$9.75
6 ft.	Per dozen	4.75	12 ft.	Per dozen	12.00
8 ft.	Per dozen	7.25	14 ft.	Per dozen	18.00

No. 742 California Style, 6 Plait, Well Made, Buck Snap.

5 ft.	Per dozen	$4.00	10 ft.	Per dozen	$13.00
6 ft.	Per dozen	5.00	12 ft.	Per dozen	16.50
8 ft.	Per dozen	9.00	14 ft.	Per dozen	20.00

Lashes—continued

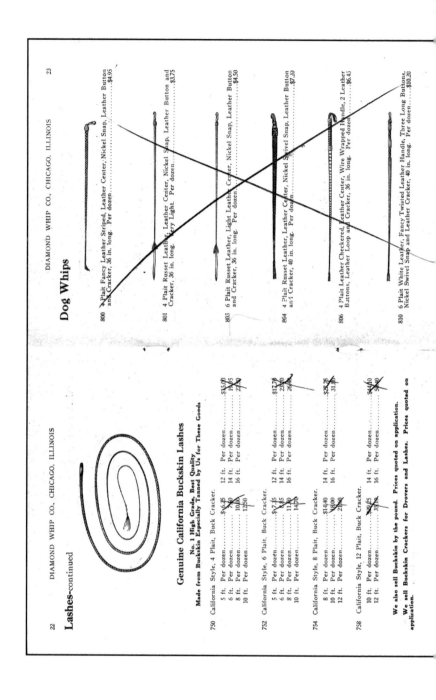

Genuine California Buckskin Lashes

No. 1 High Grade, Best Quality
Made from Buckskin Especially Tanned by Us for These Goods

750 California Style, 4 Plait, Buck Cracker.

5 ft. Per dozen....$8.45		12 ft. Per dozen....$15.00
6 ft. Per dozen....		14 ft. Per dozen....19.25
8 ft. Per dozen....10.00		16 ft. Per dozen....22.50
10 ft. Per dozen....12.50		

752 California Style, 6 Plait, Buck Cracker.

5 ft. Per dozen....$7.45		12 ft. Per dozen....$12.70
6 ft. Per dozen....		14 ft. Per dozen....23.00
8 ft. Per dozen....11.50		16 ft. Per dozen....26.00
10 ft. Per dozen....14.70		

754 California Style, 8 Plait, Buck Cracker.

8 ft. Per dozen....$14.40		14 ft. Per dozen....$27.75
10 ft. Per dozen....18.00		16 ft. Per dozen....31.50
12 ft. Per dozen....21.00		

758 California Style, 12 Plait, Buck Cracker.

10 ft. Per dozen....$20.65		14 ft. Per dozen....$34.00
12 ft. Per dozen....33.00		16 ft. Per dozen....50.00

We also sell Buckskin by the pound. Prices quoted on application.

We sell Buckskin Crackers for Drovers and Lashes. Prices quoted on application.

Dog Whips

800   4 Plait Fancy Leather Striped, Leather Center, Nickel Snap, Leather Button and Cracker, 36 in. long. Per dozen....$4.95

801   4 Plait Russet Leather, Leather Center, Nickel Snap, Leather Button and Cracker, 36 in. long, Very Light. Per dozen....$3.75

803   6 Plait Russet Leather, Light Leather Center, Nickel Snap, Leather Button and Cracker, 36 in. long. Per dozen....$4.50

804   4 Plait Russet Leather, Leather Center, Nickel Swivel Snap, Leather Button and Cracker, 40 in. long. Per dozen....$7.20

806   4 Plait Leather Checkered, Leather Center, Wire Wrapped Handle, 2 Leather Buttons, Leather Loop and Cracker, 36 in. long. Per dozen....$6.45

810   6 Plait White Leather, Fancy Twisted Leather Handle, Three Long Buttons, Nickel Swivel Snap and Leather Cracker, 40 in. long. Per dozen....$10.23

Dog Whips-continued

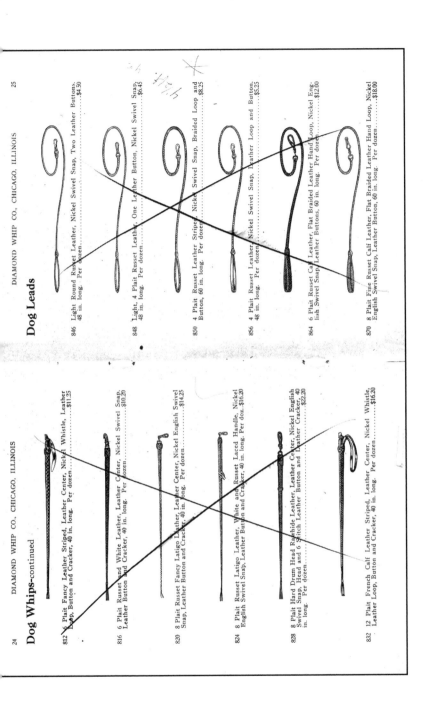

812 6 Plait Fancy Leather, Striped, Leather Center, Nickel Whistle, Leather Loop, Button and Cracker, 40 in. long. Per dozen.............$11.25

816 6 Plait Russet and White Leather, Leather Center, Nickel Swivel Snap, Leather Button and Cracker, 40 in. long. Per dozen.............$10.20

820 8 Plait Russet Fancy Latigo Leather, Leather Center, Nickel English Swivel Snap, Leather Button and Cracker, 40 in. long. Per dozen.............$14.25

824 8 Plait Russet Latigo Leather, White and Russet Laced Handle, Nickel English Swivel Snap, Leather Button and Cracker, 40 in. long. Per doz. $16.20

828 8 Plait Hard Drum Head Rawhide Leather, Leather Center, Nickel English Swivel Snap, Head and 6 Stitch Leather Button and Leather Cracker, 40 in. long. Per dozen.............$22.20

832 12 Plait French Calf Leather Striped, Leather Center, Nickel Whistle, Leather Loop, Button and Cracker, 40 in. long. Per dozen.............$16.20

Dog Leads

846 Light Round Russet Leather, Nickel Swivel Snap, Two Leather Buttons, 48 in. long. Per dozen.............$4.50

848 Light, 4 Plait Russet Leather, One Leather Button, Nickel Swivel Snap, 48 in. long. Per dozen.............$6.45

850 4 Plait Russet Leather Striped, Nickel Swivel Snap, Braided Loop and Button, 60 in. long. Per dozen.............$8.25

856 4 Plait Russet Leather Nickel Swivel Snap, Leather Loop and Button, 48 in. long. Per dozen.............$5.25

864 6 Plait Russet Calf Leather, Flat Braided Leather Hand Loop, Nickel English Swivel Snap, Leather Buttons, 60 in. long. Per dozen.............$12.00

870 8 Plait Fine Russet Calf Leather, Flat Braided Leather Hand Loop, Nickel English Swivel Snap, Leather Button, 60 in. long. Per dozen.............$18.00

Face Nets

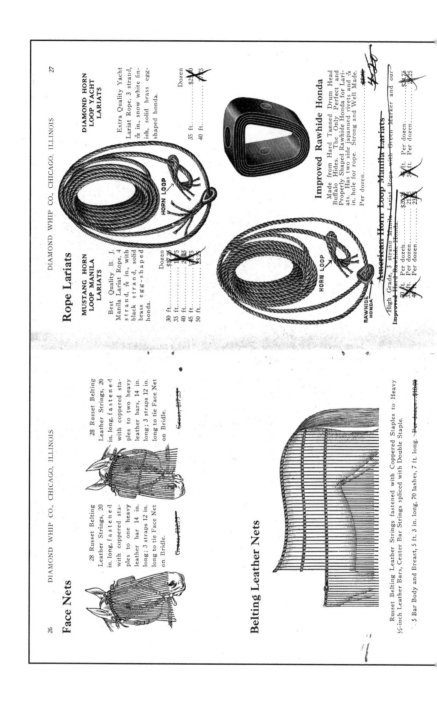

28 Russet Belting Leather Strings, 20 in. long, fastened with coppered staples to one heavy leather bar, 14 in. long; 3 straps 12 in. long to tie the Face Net on Bridle.

28 Russet Belting Leather Strings, 20 in. long, fastened with coppered staples to two heavy leather bars, 14 in. long; 3 straps 12 in. long to tie the Face Net on Bridle.

Belting Leather Nets

Russet Belting Leather Strings fastened with Coppered Staples to Heavy ½-inch Leather Bars, Center Bar Strings spliced with Double Staple.

5 Bar Body and Breast, 5 ft. 3 in. long, 70 lashes, 7 ft. long .... Per doz..... $16.00

Rope Lariats

MUSTANG HORN LOOP MANILA LARIATS

Best Quality B. J. Manila Lariat Rope, 4 strand, ⅜ in, with black strand, solid brass egg-shaped honda.

	Dozen
30 ft.	$17.25
35 ft.	19.25
40 ft.	21.25
45 ft.	23.25
50 ft.	25.25

DIAMOND HORN LOOP YACHT LARIATS

Extra Quality Yacht Lariat Rope, 3 strand, ⅜ in, snow white finish, solid brass egg-shaped honda.

	Dozen
35 ft.	$23.50
40 ft.	25.75

Improved Rawhide Honda

Made from Hard Tanned Drum Head Buffalo Hides. The Only Perfect and Properly Shaped Rawhide Honda for Lariats. Has two side japanned rivets and ⅜ in. hole for rope. Strong and Well Made.

Per dozen..........

American Horn Loop Manila Lariats

High Grade, 3 strand Manila Lariat Rope, with Green marker and our Improved Hard Rawhide Honda.

30 ft.	Per dozen	$19.25
35 ft.	Per dozen	21.25
40 ft.	Per dozen	23.25

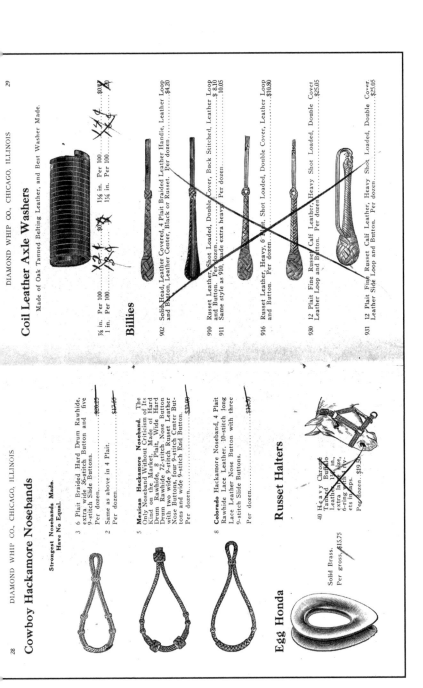

Cowboy Hackamore Nosebands

**Strongest Nosebands Made.
Have No Equal.**

3   6 Plait Braided Hard Rawhide, extra wide 36-stitch Button and five 9-stitch Side Buttons. Per dozen.................$2.25

2   Same as above in 4 Plait. Per dozen.................$1.50

5   **Mexican Hackamore Noseband.** The Only Noseband Without Criticism of Its Kind on the Market. Made of Hard Drum Rawhide, 8 Plait, Wide Hard Drum Rawhide 72-stitch Nose Button with two wide 9-stitch Russet Leather Nose Buttons, four 9-stitch Center Buttons and wide 9-stitch End Button. Per dozen.................$10.00

8   **Colorado** Hackamore Noseband, 4 Plait Rawhide Lace Leather. 10-stitch long Lace Leather Nose Button with three 9-stitch Side Buttons. Per dozen.................$4.20

Russet Halters

40 Heavy Chrome Tanned Buffalo Leather, 1 in., extra large size, 6-ring with rivets in caps. Per dozen. $19.50

Egg Honda

Solid Brass. Per gross, $15.75

Coil Leather Axle Washers

Made of Oak Tanned Belting Leather, and Best Washer Made.

¾ in. Per 100 ....$0.90
1 in. Per 100 ....
1⅜ in. Per 100 ....
1¼ in. Per 100 ....

Billies

902 Solid Head, Leather Covered, 4 Plait Braided Leather Handle, Leather Loop and Button, Leather Center, Black or Russet. Per dozen.................$4.20

910 Russet Leather, Shot Loaded, Double Cover, Buck Stitched, Leather Loop and Button. Per dozen.................$ 8.10

911 Same style as 910, made extra heavy. Per dozen.................10.05

916 Russet Leather, Heavy, 6 Plait, Shot Loaded, Double Cover, Leather Loop and Button. Per dozen.................$10.80

930 12 Plait Fine Russet Calf Leather, Heavy Shot Loaded, Double Cover, Leather Loop and Button. Per dozen.................$25.05

931 12 Plait Fine Russet Calf Leather, Heavy Shot Loaded, Double Cover, Leather Side Loop and Button. Per dozen.................$25.05

References

shford, W. G. Whips and Whipmaking. Birmingham. 1893.

unbar, Seymour. *A History of Travel in America.* New York: Tudor ublishing Company. 1937.

bbins, H. de B. *Industry in England.* London: Methuen & Co. 10.

cht, Walter. *Industrializing America.* Baltimore and London: The hn Hopkins University Press. 1995.

ayr, Otto and Robert C. Post, eds. *Yankee Enterprise.* Washington C: Smithsonian Institute Press. 1981.

cGaw, Judith A., ed. *Early American Technology.* Chapel Hill and ondon: University of North Carolina Press. 1994.

orth, Douglass C. *The Economic Growth of the United States 790-1860.* New York: W.W. Norton & Company, Inc. 1966.

hultz, Wally E. "The Nation's Only Australian Whipmaker." *The raftsman* 9, no. 2 (1965).

ommer, M. *The Shaker Garden Seed Industry.* New York: The Shaker luseum. 1972.

earight, T. B. *The Old Pike.* Uniontown, PA 1844.

owell, Thomas. *Black Rednecks and White Liberals.* San Francisco: ncounter Books. 2005.

Simons, A. M. *Social Forces in American History.* New York: Macmilla
Company. 1912.

The Carriage Journal, no. 1. Summer 1973.

"Whips Crack in Southfield." *Southfield Berkshire Eagle.* February
1964.

About the Author

An engineer by training and vocation, David W. Morgan was born and raised in Canada. He attended graduate school in England and while there, met his future wife, an Australian. The couple married, returned to Canada, and shortly thereafter emigrated to the United States.

David Morgan developed an interest in leather braiding and whipmaking during a visit to Australia in 1961. At that time, stockmen were still using whips to work range cattle, and there was a viable, though diminishing, craft industry producing whips. After returning to the United States, the author and his wife set up a part-time mail-order business which sold, among other things, Australian whips to American stuntmen and cattlemen. This allowed David Morgan to develop his interest in whipmaking. Later, an embargo on the importation of kangaroo products into the United States prompted him to make whips in order to maintain a supply to sell. His American-style bullwhip was used in the Indiana Jones movies, which sparked a revival of interest in whips and whipcracking and produced a continuing demand for the whip used in these movies. Production of this whip gave him an understanding of the practical aspects of the trade and a deeper appreciation of the skills of the older craftsmen.

Over time, the mail-order business expanded in size and scope, and it became a full-time occupation. However, the author has maintained his interest in leather craft, actively braiding as well as attempting to record the history of whips, insofar as it may still be possible to do so.

Cornell Maritime Press